Acting Duets for

YOUNG WOMEN

8 to 10 minute duo scenes for practice and competition

Laurie Allen

MERIWETHER PUBL
Colorado Springs,

Meriwether Publishing Ltd., Publisher
PO Box 7710
Colorado Springs, CO 80933-7710

www.meriwether.com

Editor: Theodore O. Zapel
Assistant editor: Amy Hammelev
Cover design: Jan Melvin

Library of Congress Cataloging-in-Publication Data

Allen, Laurie, 1962-
    Acting duets for young women : eight- to ten-minute duo scenes for
practice and competition / by Laurie Allen. -- 1st ed.
        p. cm.
    ISBN 978-1-56608-172-6
    1. Dialogues--Juvenile literature. 2. Acting--Auditions--Juvenile
literature. 3. Teenage girls--Drama--Juvenile literature. I. Title.
    PN2080.A43 2010
    792.02'8082--dc22
                                            2010022785

        1   2   3   10   11   12

Table of Contents

Comedy

1. Showstopper

Cast: EMILY and CARMEN
Setting: The set of *Shopping on Television*

1   *(At rise, EMILY faces the audience. The camera light comes on*
2   *and she begins, exhibiting much excitement.)*
3   **EMILY: Hello, everyone! Hello! Welcome to S-O-T, *Shopping on***
4   **   *Television!* I'm Emily Duncan, and we have such an**
5   **   exciting hour in front of us today! I'm so excited! Because in**
6   **   a moment, I'm going to introduce to you my absolute**
7   **   favorite pick of the day! If you're looking for quality, style,**
8   **   and fashion, then ladies, this is a must! Pay attention, this**
9   **   is our showstopper! Our very own, exclusive, made for**
10 **   S-O-T fashion design that is going to fly right out of here! If**
11 **   you don't love it, well ... there's no way you couldn't love this**
12 **   one-of-a-kind, absolutely gorgeous jacket. Made in the USA,**
13 **   it's figure-flattering and washer friendly. And best of all,**
14 **   ladies, this jacket will make you appear as if you just**
15 **   walked out of the most expensive department store. And**
16 **   who doesn't want that look? So here, to introduce to you**
17 **   our very first ever, exclusive outerwear by designer Fabian**
18 **   Fields is our model Carmen. *(Claps.)* Carmen, welcome!**
19 **CARMEN: *(Enters.)* Hello, holidays! Hello, fashion color!**
20 **EMILY: Fabulous! Absolutely fabulous! This is a must have for**
21 **   the season. And if you would notice —**
22 **CARMEN: It's so lightweight, yet keeps you plenty warm.**
23 **EMILY: Thank you, Carmen. Ladies, lightweight is so important**
24 **   because you don't want to be driving around in a big, bulky**
25 **   jacket.**
26 **CARMEN: No, because big, bulky jackets can be so restricting.**

1   But this ... *(Twirls)* fall fashion and fall comfort all in one!

2   Not to mention that it's designed by the legendary Fabian

3   Fields!

4 EMILY: Carmen, if you would just step back so that the

5   audience can have a clear view. Yes, elegant and feminine.

6   Now, ladies, let's talk about the colors.

7 CARMEN: Today's exclusive jacket comes in three amazing

8   colors.

9 EMILY: Carmen, I'll tell the audience about the colors we offer.

10 CARMEN: *(Quickly)* Classic black, midnight blue, and glam red!

11 EMILY: Ladies, as you can see, we offer three great color

12   choices.

13 CARMEN: Three!

14 EMILY: Classic black —

15 CARMEN: *(Quickly)* Midnight blue and glam red!

16 EMILY: Thank you, Carmen. I'll take it from here. If you would

17   just step back, please. Camera, let's zoom in right here on

18   me as I tell you more about this exclusive Fabian Fields

19   jacket. Now, let's talk about the sizes that are available.

20 CARMEN: Let's.

21 EMILY: Ladies, this adorable jacket designed by our own

22   Fabian Fields is offered in a wide range of sizes.

23 CARMEN: Petite, missy, or plus size.

24 EMILY: Carmen, let us remember that you're the model and

25   I'm the host. Now the sizes available are petite, missy, or

26   plus size.

27 CARMEN: In extra small through extra, extra large. I'm

28   wearing the extra small.

29 EMILY: Extra small?

30 CARMEN: *(Smiles at the camera.)* Yes, I wear extra small. But as

31   I mentioned, plus size is also available.

32 EMILY: Yes, our customers will be pleased to know the variety

33   of sizes that are available. But Carmen, you know you're

34   not wearing an extra small.

35 CARMEN: Yes, I am! This is an extra small.

1   EMILY: Why do you always do this?

2   CARMEN: *(Smiling at the camera)* Always do what?

3   EMILY: Ruin my show.

4   CARMEN: How do I ruin your show?

5   EMILY: For one thing, you're lying to the audience. That is not

6   an extra small.

7   CARMEN: Yes it is! *(Turns.)* Slimming, isn't it?

8   EMILY: Well, if that were an extra small, I'd hate to see the

9   extra, extra large.

10   CARMEN: As usual, Emily, your jealous side is showing.

11   EMILY: I'm not jealous. I'm truthful. And I don't believe in

12   being deceptive to our wonderful audience out there.

13   CARMEN: No? Excuse me, but I'm the only one around here

14   who speaks up when I think we're selling bad products on

15   the show!

16   EMILY: And you think this Fabian Fields jacket is a bad

17   product?

18   CARMEN: I didn't say that, did I?

19   EMILY: Carmen, may I remind you that your job is to model the

20   products we sell. We don't need your input here.

21   CARMEN: I'm just trying to help.

22   EMILY: You're not helping. Believe me.

23   CARMEN: So you want me to just stand here?

24   EMILY: Yes! That's your job, Carmen. To just stand there! Now

25   ladies, I have to tell you that this Fabian Fields jacket will

26   sell out in no time, so pick up those phones and place that

27   order. Again, the colors available are —

28   CARMEN: Classic black, midnight blue, and glam red!

29   EMILY: And the sizes available are —

30   CARMEN: Extra small through extra, extra large!

31   EMILY: And so slimming, you will *feel* as if you're wearing the

32   extra small.

33   CARMEN: Which I am.

34   EMILY: But in reality, the larger, more comfortable jacket that

35   Carmen is wearing is quite flattering for the big and

1   **beautiful woman.**

2   **CARMEN: Big and beautiful? Excuse me, Emily! I'm a size two!**

3   **EMILY:** *(Laughs.)* **Please!**

4   **CARMEN: Oh, here you go again!**

5   **EMILY: What do you mean,** *here I go again?!*

6   **CARMEN: Trying to draw the attention away from the model**

7   **and to you! Emily, I am the model. The cameras are on me,**

8   **not you!**

9   **EMILY: Look here, Carmen! I'm selling the product here! It's**

10   **my description and my excitement over this item that**

11   **makes those phones ring and gets those orders placed!**

12   **CARMEN: Do you want to know what excitement is?**

13   **EMILY: You don't have to tell me! Excitement is my middle**

14   **name! And ladies, who wouldn't be excited over this Fabian**

15   **Fields jacket?**

16   **CARMEN: Zoom in on me, cameraman! Because I'm the one**

17   **wearing the exclusive, never-before-offered, one-of-a-kind**

18   **product that is available only on S-O-T!**

19   **EMILY: Once again, Carmen, let me remind you what your job**

20   **description is! Your job is to stand there and smile. That's**

21   **it! Just smile!**

22   **CARMEN: Which is exactly what I'm doing! Smiling!** *(Smiles at*

23   *the camera.)*

24   **EMILY: And I'll do all the talking. So if you would just step back**

25   **a bit. A little further please. Carmen, please step back.**

26   **CARMEN:** *(Steps forward.)* **Yes, this exclusive Fabian Fields**

27   **jackets is a must. Affordable and fashionable.**

28   **EMILY: Step back and shut up!**

29   **CARMEN: Shall we mention the prices?**

30   **EMILY: I'll mention the prices, Carmen!**

31   **CARMEN: So let me tell you about the tremendous value we're**

32   **offering on this weekend surprise.**

33   **EMILY: Carmen, this is my weekend surprise!**

34   **CARMEN: A first-time offer available only on S-O-T.**

35   **EMILY: Step back and let me tell our audience about our**

1   first-time offer!

2   **CARMEN: Three easy payments of thirty-nine ninety-nine.**

3   **EMILY: Stop it, Carmen!** *(Smiles at the camera.)* **Three easy**

4   **payments of thirty-nine ninety-nine.**

5   **CARMEN: Never offered before on Easy Pay.**

6   **EMILY: It's today's special value pick.** *(Twirls.)* **Your weekend**

7   **surprise!**

8   **CARMEN: So to take advantage of this exclusive offer —**

9   **EMILY: That's my line, Carmen! So, to take advantage of this of**

10   **this exclusive offer —**

11   **CARMEN: Call the one eight hundred number on your screen**

12   **or shop with us online within the next thirty minutes.**

13   **EMILY: Will you shut up! Just shut up! I'm the host and you're**

14   **the model!**

15   **CARMEN: A model with many talents. Beauty, brains, and**

16   **talent, all wrapped up in an extra small.**

17   **EMILY: I have an idea. Why don't you take the jacket off and I'll**

18   **take it from here! Crew, bring me a mannequin!** *Now!*

19   **CARMEN: You mean you'd rather have a mannequin over a**

20   **beautiful model?**

21   **EMILY:** *(To the crew)* **What? We don't have one available? Then**

22   **find me one! Now!** *(Pause)* **Then I'll use Harold! Harold, get**

23   **over here and put this jacket on!**

24   **CARMEN: Excuse me, but I'm wearing this jacket!**

25   **EMILY: Take it off! Harold!** *(Motioning for him to come up to the*

26   *stage)*

27   **CARMEN: Don't do it, Harold! It wouldn't look good on you!**

28   **EMILY: Take the jacket off, Carmen!**

29   **CARMEN: No!**

30   **EMILY: And if they can't find a mannequin and Harold refuses**

31   **to step up here on the stage, then ... then I'll stand here and**

32   **hold the jacket up for our audience to see!**

33   **CARMEN: Emily, I'm not taking it off! I want to wear it!** *(Smiles*

34   *at the camera.)* **Hello, holidays! Hello, fashion color!**

35   **EMILY: Why? Why do you always have to ruin my show?**

1   **CARMEN: Ruin your show? When did I ever ruin your show?**

2   **EMILY: Let's see ... how about last Tuesday?**

3   **CARMEN: Last Tuesday? What happened last Tuesday?**

4   **EMILY: When I was selling the Super Soft Pillows.**

5   **CARMEN: Emily, I did not model the Super Soft Pillows.**

6   **EMILY: No, but you were the person who phoned in as our**

7   **pretend customer.**

8   **CARMEN: Oh, that. Now I remember. I called in to the show as**

9   **Shirley from Delaware.**

10 **EMILY: And do you remember how the producer insisted on us**

11   **selling two thousand of those Super Soft Pillows? Two**

12   **thousand were to be sold during that fifteen-minute time**

13   **frame!**

14 **CARMEN: Uh, Emily, selling the Super Soft Pillows was your**

15   **job, not mine. I was just the pretend customer, remember?**

16 **EMILY: Yes, and the show was going great.** *(Smiles at the*

17   *camera.)* **For a great night's sleep, these big, oversized**

18   **pillows are so comfy, so soft, and so luxurious. Surround**

19   **yourself with unbelievable comfort. Because believe me,**

20   **you will not find a better quality pillow. So, if you already**

21   **have one of these pillows, please call us on our testimonial**

22   **line.**

23 **CARMEN: Hello.**

24 **EMILY: And who am I speaking to?**

25 **CARMEN: This is Shirley from Delaware.**

26 **EMILY: Hello, Shirley from Delaware! Do you own one of these**

27   **Super Soft Pillows?**

28 **CARMEN: No I don't.**

29 **EMILY:** *(Turns to CARMEN.)* **You were supposed to say yes!**

30 **CARMEN: I didn't want to lie!**

31 **EMILY:** *(Back to smiling at camera)* **No? Well, uh ... let me remind**

32   **you, Shirley, that a great day begins with a good night's**

33   **sleep!**

34 **CARMEN: Actually, a great day begins with a good breakfast.**

35 **EMILY: After a good night's sleep! And with these limited**

1   edition Super Soft Pillows —

2   CARMEN: You know, those oversized pillows are just a little too

3   big if you ask me.

4   EMILY: Too big to believe, isn't it? Yes, hard to believe that this

5   oversized pillow is as comfortable as it looks!

6   CARMEN: Which would seriously hurt my neck. Talk about

7   waking up with a crick in your neck! You know, I prefer

8   sleeping on a nice flat pillow.

9   EMILY: And thank you for the call, Shirley from Delaware.

10   *(Turns to CARMEN.)* Do you know how many pillows I sold?

11   Two! *Two!*

12   CARMEN: I'm sorry. For some reason I forgot I was on TV.

13   EMILY: Then there was yesterday.

14   CARMEN: Which yesterday the producer said I should stick to

15   modeling. No more setting me up as pretend customers

16   with online testimonials.

17   EMILY: Talk about a nightmare!

18   CARMEN: I wouldn't exactly call it a nightmare.

19   EMILY: *(To audience)* Ladies, our Magic Lip Color is what's in

20   store for you today. Five high quality lipsticks for our

21   special introductory price of only thirty-eight fifty.

22   Gorgeous colors in wine, rose, berry, mahogany, and raisin.

23   CARMEN: I prefer a shimmery pale color.

24   EMILY: We're going to the phones now. Hi, you're live on the

25   air. Who am I speaking to?

26   CARMEN: Hi, this is Susan from Hawaii.

27   EMILY: Hello, Susan! So tell me, are you impressed with our

28   new Magic Lip Color?

29   CARMEN: Truthfully?

30   EMILY: Well, yes. Of course.

31   CARMEN: Well, truthfully, I prefer to look like a human being

32   and not like a cartoon character.

33   EMILY: And with Magic Lip Color you feel like a human, right?

34   CARMEN: No, I feel like a cartoon character. This raisin color is

35   very scary.

1 **EMILY:** *(Turns to CARMEN.)* **And thank you very much. We had**
2   **one order! One!**
3 **CARMEN: I'm sorry! Like I said, the producer agreed I should**
4   **stick to modeling.**
5 **EMILY: Right. Modeling. And models smile and don't talk. Got**
6   **it?**
7 **CARMEN: I'm smiling.**
8 **EMILY:** *(Looks at the camera, smiles. A pause)* **Again, if I might**
9   **emphasize the quality of our own exclusive outerwear by**
10   **Fabian Fields. This exciting offer is only available on S-O-T**
11   **so, ladies, pick up that phone and order, because quantities**
12   **are limited.**
13 **CARMEN: Actually, we're kinda overstocked on this item. Did**
14   **you know that? They have like an extra couple thousand**
15   **that may end up on eBay if they can't move them by today.**
16   **And if that happens, instead of making three easy**
17   **payments, it'll be like one easy bargain online.**
18 **EMILY: Carmen!** *(Smiles at the camera.)* **Yes, this jacket, this**
19   **Fabian Fields jacket is a must. Fabulous, fabulous,**
20   **fabulous. And we'll be right back.** *(Turns to CARMEN and*
21   *gives her a look.)*
22 **CARMEN: What? What?**
23 **EMILY: I quit!** *(Steps back.)*
24 **CARMEN: What do you mean you quit? We're coming back on**
25   **in a couple of seconds with the Magic Lotion. Where are**
26   **you going? Someone has to be here! They can't televise an**
27   **empty stage! You're the host! You're supposed to do the**
28   **talking and I'm supposed to do the modeling. But if you're**
29   **not here ... I mean, the show can't just stop! It never stops!**
30   **We have to keep selling. Selling, selling, selling.** *(Pause. She*
31   *smiles at the camera.)* **Wrinkles and dark spots on your face?**
32   **Well, with Magic Lotion, you roll it on and they disappear.**
33   **It's a miracle lotion. A never-before-seen solution for those**
34   **bothersome brown spots and wrinkles. Forget being**
35   **embarrassed by looking old before your time. Wrinkles?**

1   Gone! Discolorations? Gone! This Magic Lotion is your
2   solution to those problems! Incredible! Unbelievable!
3   *(Looks to the side, then back at the camera.)* Well, actually, if
4   it were me, I wouldn't use this high dollar stuff! Over at the
5   dollar store, you can get this off-brand face cream that
6   works like wonders! Trust me!
7
8
9
10
11
12
13
14
15
16
17
18
19
20
21
22
23
24
25
26
27
28
29
30
31
32
33
34
35

2. Online Love

Cast: NICOLE and ALANA
Setting: A wedding reception

1 NICOLE: So, are you here for the bride or the groom?

2 ALANA: The groom. He's my date's cousin. Who seems to have
3   disappeared. Oh, there he is. *(Points.)* He's over there at
4   the buffet table. Actually, he's just a guy I'm friends with.
5   He didn't want to come to the wedding alone. And being
6   the nice person that I am ... What about you? The bride or
7   the groom?

8 NICOLE: The groom. He's my ... uh, ex.

9 ALANA: Your ex?

10 NICOLE: Yes. My ex-boyfriend.

11 ALANA: Oh! Wow. You two remained friends, huh? That's nice
12   he invited you to his wedding.

13 NICOLE: He didn't.

14 ALANA: He didn't? You mean you're crashing your ex-
15   boyfriend's wedding?

16 NICOLE: *(Leans over.)* I'm wearing a wig. That way he won't
17   recognize me.

18 ALANA: A wig? But your hair looks so real.

19 NICOLE: I know. I'm really a blonde. *(Or any other color)*

20 ALANA: And I bet you don't wear glasses either, do you?

21 NICOLE: That's correct. I borrowed these from a friend. And
22   I'm having the hardest time seeing through them. *(Peers
23   over the glasses.)* But I can clearly see that Mario will be
24   miserable with ... with ... whatever her name is.

25 ALANA: Abby. And why do you say that?

26 NICOLE: Because I know Mario better than she does.

1   ALANA: Are you sure? I mean, he did choose to marry Abby.
2   Surely they know each other fairly well. And Mario told
3   Clyde, my date, that he and Abby fell in love the moment
4   they met each other.
5   NICOLE: Oh, really? And where did they meet?
6   ALANA: He didn't tell you?
7   NICOLE: No.
8   ALANA: At the Frisco Deli.
9   NICOLE: *(Sarcastic)* Wow. How romantic.
10 ALANA: Apparently they were each ordering shaved peppered
11   ham and it was this moment where they both looked over
12   and ... well, they've been in love ever since.
13 NICOLE: You're telling me that Mario and Abby fell in love over
14   shaved peppered ham?
15 ALANA: Apparently. Well, that's what I heard. So you really
16   loved Mario?
17 NICOLE: Yes. Mario and I were the perfect match. Well, we're
18   still the perfect match.
19 ALANA: I hate to ask you this, but you're not stalking him, are
20   you? Because you know, you can get into a lot of serious
21   trouble for doing that. Maybe even arrested and go to jail.
22 NICOLE: No! I'm not stalking him!
23 ALANA: Oh, well I guess you just had to see it for yourself, huh?
24   I guess it's like closure for you. Kind of like when you see
25   a dead person in a casket. Suddenly you realize they are
26   really dead. Now, looking across the room at your ex-
27   boyfriend with his lovely bride, you have to realize that
28   he's married and the relationship is over.
29 NICOLE: *(Moves glasses down on nose.)* Not necessarily.
30 ALANA: Look! They're cutting the cake. I wonder if he's going
31   to gently feed her that piece of wedding cake or smear it
32   all over her face. *(They watch.)* Aw ... that was sweet.
33 NICOLE: He's fooling himself, that's what he's doing.
34 ALANA: Oh, look! Abby got him good! *(Laughs.)* Man, it's all over
35   his face! Well, at least he's laughing. And look how she's

1   licking the icing off his cheek. That's cute. Oh, I wish I had
2   my camera.
3   NICOLE: And then he's going to wake up tomorrow and
4   remember our special date.
5   ALANA: What? You have a date with the groom tomorrow?
6   NICOLE: I do.
7   ALANA: How can that be? Mario is going to be in Jamaica on his
8   honeymoon with his beautiful bride. He can't leave to go
9   on a date with you. It must be a misunderstanding.
10 NICOLE: Oh, it's no misunderstanding. Mario and I agreed to
11   meet at The Liberty Bridge on June third every year ... no
12   matter what. And tomorrow is June third.
13 ALANA: I'm sure that was a romantic promise you both made
14   at one time, but obviously the circumstances have
15   changed.
16 NICOLE: I still plan to show up at The Liberty Bridge
17   tomorrow.
18 ALANA: You know, you may be waiting for a long time.
19 NICOLE: I'd wait forever for Mario.
20 ALANA: So how many times have you and Mario met at The
21   Liberty Bridge?
22 NICOLE: How many times?
23 ALANA: You said you agreed to meet every year. How many
24   years have you met him there?
25 NICOLE: Well, tomorrow was going to be our first time there.
26 ALANA: Your first?
27 NICOLE: Yes.
28 ALANA: Oh. So, how long were you two together?
29 NICOLE: Tomorrow would have been a year.
30 ALANA: I'm sorry. Sometimes things just don't work out. I've
31   been there myself. I know it can be painful.
32 NICOLE: But we shared so much! I mean, we shared
33   everything! All day, all night ...
34 ALANA: Wow. Sounds like you two were inseparable.
35 NICOLE: Yes. We were constantly sending each other instant

1   messages, e-mails ... I should text him right now and see if
2   he responds.
3 ALANA: Uh, I wouldn't do that.
4 NICOLE: I won't tell him I'm here. I'll just say ... let's see, what
5   shall I say?
6 ALANA: How about, "Hope you're happy. Wishing you the
7   best!"
8 NICOLE: How about, "I still love you, Mario!"
9 ALANA: I don't think that's a good idea. On his wedding day
10   and all ... So where did you and Mario meet?
11 NICOLE: Online.
12 ALANA: You met online?
13 NICOLE: Yes. It's been the best long distance relationship that
14   I've ever had. And I'd say after about the third e-mail, we
15   were in love. Mario said that. Third e-mail. *Nicole, I'm*
16   *falling in love with you.*
17 ALANA: Really? So how long was it until you and Mario met?
18   When you went on your first *real* date?
19 NICOLE: Oh, we never met. I live in Phoenix and he lives here
20   in Greenville.
21 ALANA: You never met? Are you serious?
22 NICOLE: Well, it depends on what your definition of met is. We
23   met on the Internet. That's where we fell in love. But did
24   we actually meet in person? Like over shaved peppered
25   ham? No. But I can tell you this: Mario and I shared our
26   deepest feelings with each other over the last several
27   months. And I know him better than she does!
28 ALANA: Uh, question. If you and Mario never actually met,
29   then why are you wearing a disguise?
30 NICOLE: Because he knows what I look like! We sent each other
31   pictures!
32 ALANA: And you came to his wedding to ... ?
33 NICOLE: To see this for myself!
34 ALANA: Well, it's good to face the truth so you can close this
35   chapter of your life and move on.

1   NICOLE: What's good is to find the courage ...

2   ALANA: To do what?

3   NICOLE: To walk over there and face him.

4   ALANA: Oh no! That's not a good idea! Not here! Not at his

5   wedding! I think you should just go home and e-mail him.

6   Yes! Write him a long e-mail and tell him exactly how you

7   feel!

8   NICOLE: So I can remind Mario of the past year we spent

9   together?

10 ALANA: Uh ... I believe you spent the past year apart. You in

11   Phoenix and him here in Greenville. Remember? And in

12   the meantime, he was at the deli falling in love with his

13   beautiful bride.

14 NICOLE: Mario needs to be reminded of how I was there for

15   him. And how he was there for me. We shared everything.

16   Our hurts, our fears, our passions, our love ...

17 ALANA: Look, he's moved on.

18 NICOLE: No, you don't understand! Until last week, I was the

19   love of his life!

20 ALANA: You two were still talking online until last week?

21 NICOLE: Until he confessed. All this time ... all this time he's

22   been carrying on with her!

23 ALANA: Uh ... she's his wife now.

24 NICOLE: Granted, I was not within his reach, but he didn't have

25   to go to the deli and lie to me about it!

26 ALANA: So how did you find out about him getting married

27   today?

28 NICOLE: Well, last week he sent me an e-mail and confessed to

29   me that he had not been truthful with me. Or faithful for

30   that matter. He told me he was getting married the

31   following Saturday and could no longer correspond with

32   me.

33 ALANA: I see. Well, I'm sure that was hard after you'd invested

34   so much time into the relationship.

35 NICOLE: It was.

1 ALANA: And in all truthfulness, it wasn't fair to either one of

2   you. He shouldn't have been proclaiming his love to you

3   while making plans to marry Abby. Even if the two of you

4   never had met, it still wasn't right.

5 NICOLE: Exactly! So after one year of dating online, he does

6   this to me? Like he can just delete me like a piece of spam

7   mail?

8 ALANA: Wow! I hope Mario doesn't do the same thing to Abby.

9 NICOLE: So ... I made a copy of every e-mail he ever sent to me.

10 ALANA: You did?

11 NICOLE: You better believe I did! One for me ... and one for her!

12 ALANA: Here? You brought it here?

13 NICOLE: I sure did. See that wrapped gift on the table over

14   there with the red ribbon around it?

15 ALANA: You didn't?!

16 NICOLE: I did. But then I thought if Mario would agree to walk

17   out of here with me ...

18 ALANA: And leave his wife?

19 NICOLE: It's time for him to choose.

20 ALANA: But he did choose!

21 NICOLE: No. He's confused.

22 ALANA: Well, his cousin, my date, did say that he almost backed

23   out. Something about not being sure if he wanted to give

24   up his freedom ...

25 NICOLE: See! He was confused!

26 ALANA: Maybe ...

27 NICOLE: So if he sees me ...

28 ALANA: If he sees you he'll probably have his best man whisk

29   you away, tie you up, and throw you in the back of a van

30   until they leave for their honeymoon.

31 NICOLE: No. I think if he sees me he'll realize that it's me who

32   he really wants. Not her. And we can jump into my car and

33   speed away. And we can live happily ever after.

34 ALANA: And if he wants to stay with her?

35 NICOLE: Then let him stay! *(Peers over he glasses.)* But that deli

1   **chick doesn't know what we've shared for the past year.**
2   **Because I'm the one who held him together when his**
3   **sister passed away. And when he lost his job at the**
4   **convenience store, I was the one who was there for him.**
5   **And when the bank hired him and immediately promoted**
6   **him to vice president, it was me who praised him for his**
7   **accomplishments. We drank champagne and talked on**
8   **the phone all night long.**
9   **ALANA: Vice president of the bank?**
10   **NICOLE: That's my Mario. Vice president of the bank.**
11   **ALANA: Mario, your groom over there?**
12   **NICOLE: Yes. My one true love.**
13   **ALANA: Uh ... he's a teller at the bank, but not the vice**
14   **president.**
15   **NICOLE: You mean he was exaggerating? Well, that silly boy.**
16   **That's OK. I still love him. And oh, he has such a way with**
17   **words. You should see some of the poems he wrote me.**
18   **Oh, I love him so much!**
19   **ALANA: But his cousin, Clyde, my date over there, he did work**
20   **at a convenience store. And he did get laid off a few**
21   **months ago.**
22   **NICOLE: What?**
23   **ALANA: And Clyde's sister did pass away about a year ago.**
24   **NICOLE: Don't you mean Mario's sister?**
25   **ALANA: No. Mario doesn't have a sister. And Mario has never**
26   **worked at a convenience store. But Clyde did.**
27   **NICOLE: What are you trying to tell me?**
28   **ALANA: Which makes me remember all those times Clyde told**
29   **me how he'd do anything to find the woman of his**
30   **dreams.**
31   **NICOLE: No! Do not tell me this!**
32   **ALANA: I don't think Clyde meant to be deceitful with you. I**
33   **think he just borrowed his cousin's name and picture so**
34   **he could impress you. I think it's because he's**
35   **embarrassed. You know, because of his weight. I think he**

1   weighs a good three hundred pounds. But how can that
2   really matter if it's the person on the inside you fell in love
3   with?
4 NICOLE: No! No! This can't be happening to me!
5 ALANA: Which means —
6 NICOLE: Which means I don't know the groom over there
7   who's dancing with his lovely wife!
8 ALANA: I'm sorry. But you know my date. Oh, there he is! He's
9   the one at the buffet table with the peppered ham
10   hanging out of his mouth.
11 NICOLE: You mean I've been talking to him?
12 ALANA: I'm afraid so. Did he tell you he likes to eat?
13 NICOLE: Yes, but ...
14 ALANA: A lot?
15 NICOLE: I can't believe this! He's the person I fell so deeply in
16   love with?
17 ALANA: He is a great guy, Nicole.
18 NICOLE: But he sounded so wonderful. Especially on the
19   phone. And he had this deep, sexy voice ...
20 ALANA: Oh, he does have a deep, sexy voice! Come on! Let's go
21   over there so you can hear it in person!
22 NICOLE: No! No!
23 ALANA: So he was a little shy to give you his real name or his
24   real photos, but Clyde is a really sweet and sexy guy when
25   you get past his obsession with food. He's just a big old
26   teddy bear! Come on! Let's go say hello. And you can tell
27   him how much you still love him!
28 NICOLE: No!
29 ALANA: What's wrong?
30 NICOLE: *(Takes off glasses.)* You mean ... you mean I fell in love
31   with that face?
32 ALANA: The groom is quite handsome, isn't he?
33 NICOLE: But the person I was talking to ... *(Points)* was him? Mr.
34   Teddy Bear?
35 ALANA: Wow. He's still eating. He must really be hungry. Hey,

1   where are you going?

2   NICOLE: To get my wedding present back!

3   ALANA: But —

4   NICOLE: No point in the groom having his day ruined over

5   someone else's lie!

6   ALANA: Good point! But are you sure you don't want to go over

7   there and talk to Clyde?

8   NICOLE: I'm sure! And look, we never had this conversation,

9   OK?

10   ALANA: OK, sure. No problem.

11   NICOLE: And Clyde ... well ... you can have him! *(Quickly exits.)*

12   ALANA: *(Takes a deep breath, fanning herself)* Oh, my gosh! I just

13   saved the groom from a quickie divorce. Oh! This could

14   have been a disaster! Oh, and Mario ... you're going to owe

15   me for this one! You idiot! *(Exits.)*

16

17

18

19

20

21

22

23

24

25

26

27

28

29

30

31

32

33

34

35

3. The Shot

Cast: PATIENT and NURSE
Setting: The doctor's office

1 PATIENT: *(As NURSE enters)* **Wait! I'm not ready!**
2 NURSE: Doctor Fletcher told me I'd have a problem with you.
3   Look. Nothing in my hands.
4 PATIENT: This must seem silly to you.
5 NURSE: That you're afraid of getting a shot?
6 PATIENT: That I'm afraid of getting a shot at my age.
7 NURSE: Sweetheart, don't feel bad. I see both children and
8   adults who are petrified of injections. Even grown men.
9   Believe me, I understand.
10 PATIENT: Thank you. But it is rather embarrassing to be so
11   fearful. I bet you're not afraid of shots, are you?
12 NURSE: Me? Oh, no. I can give them and I can take them. Heck,
13   I can even give them to myself if needed.
14 PATIENT: I wish I were like you.
15 NURSE: Well, don't you worry. I'm here to calm your fears. So,
16   how long has it been since you last received a shot?
17 PATIENT: Oh, not since I was a child. I was probably seven or
18   eight years old.
19 NURSE: And it was a bad experience?
20 PATIENT: The worst.
21 NURSE: Tell me about it.
22 PATIENT: Well, this angry looking nurse entered the room,
23   proudly holding up this enormous-sized needle! And
24   when I saw that, I went nuts! I started screaming and
25   crying. They ended up having to restrain me. It took three
26   nurses and a doctor to hold me down. And the pain ... it

1   was unbearable!
2   NURSE: I'm sure as a child it seemed much worse than it
3   actually was. You know, as children, the smallest upsets
4   can seem quite huge. Like skinning a knee or getting a
5   sticker in your foot.
6   PATIENT: Oh, no! I still remember it clearly. The needle ... I'm
7   telling you, it was this long. *(Shows her.)*
8   NURSE: *(Laughs.)* Needles are never that long!
9   PATIENT: Oh, but it was! And the medicine was this thick pale
10   yellow stuff that burned like crazy when it was going in.
11   Seriously, it was the worst experience I've ever had! And I
12   don't want to repeat it.
13   NURSE: Well, our needles are this little. *(Shows her.)* And you
14   can barely feel them.
15   PATIENT: I hope you're telling me the truth.
16   NURSE: Of course I am. So, here's what I want you to do. When
17   I leave the room, I want you to look at that poster on the
18   wall. And when I come back in, just keep looking at that
19   poster, OK?
20   PATIENT: Stare at the puppy and kitten?
21   NURSE: That's right. Aren't they cute?
22   PATIENT: I guess.
23   NURSE: Then I will apply something cold to your arm.
24   PATIENT: Alcohol?
25   NURSE: Yes, that's right. And then I will tell you to take a deep
26   breath, and then you'll feel a tiny little pinch.
27   PATIENT: Please don't lie to me.
28   NURSE: I'm not lying.
29   PATIENT: Because we both know it feels worse than a tiny little
30   pinch.
31   NURSE: No it doesn't.
32   PATIENT: *(Holds out her arm.)* Show me. Show me how it will
33   feel.
34   NURSE: *(Lightly pinches her arm.)* Like this. Now that wasn't
35   bad, was it?

1 PATIENT: No. But you're lying. I know you are. If it was like
2   that, *(Pinches NURSE's arm)* then babies wouldn't scream
3   at the top of their lungs!
4 NURSE: But you're not a baby, are you? And if you do feel a little
5   sting, it will only last for a second or two. So, look at that
6   cute puppy and kitten poster and try to relax, OK?
7 PATIENT: *(Looks at the poster.)* Do you really think that a
8   picture of a puppy and kitten will calm my fears? And
9   really, if you think about it, the puppy would be growling
10   at the cat and the cat would be hissing at the puppy. And
11   then the cat would rear up and swipe the puppy's nose
12   with its sharp claws. And then the puppy would cry like
13   this. *(Demonstrates.)* And then the puppy's nose would
14   bleed, which would probably feel similar to the pain of
15   the shot you are about to give me. Then the kitten would
16   run away and the puppy would continue to sit there and
17   cry in pain. And well, truthfully, I don't think that's a very
18   calming picture after all.
19 NURSE: That was a bit much, don't you think?
20 PATIENT: It's just what I see. Poor little puppy.
21 NURSE: Then why don't you close your eyes and think of
22   something pleasant? Maybe imagine yourself on a beach,
23   lying on the warm sand.
24 PATIENT: I don't particularly like the ocean. My friend's uncle
25   had his leg bitten off by a shark. Since then, I stay out of
26   the water.
27 NURSE: I said you were on the warm sand, not in the water.
28 PATIENT: And I also try to stay out of the sun. I don't care to
29   wrinkle up at an early age. You know?
30 NURSE: Then how about the mountains?
31 PATIENT: Is there snow?
32 NURSE: Yes! Snow-covered mountains. Clean, brisk air.
33   Calming. Refreshing.
34 PATIENT: What am I doing on the snow-covered mountain?
35 NURSE: I don't know ...

1   PATIENT: Am I lost? I hiked up the mountain and lost my way?

2   Search parties are out looking for me? Helicopters are

3   above me, but somehow they can't see me? Frostbite has

4   set in and I'll be lucky if I get to keep my fingers and toes.

5   That is, if they find me.

6   NURSE: No! You're sitting outside a log cabin as you enjoy the

7   fresh air, the clean snow, and the sounds of nature.

8   PATIENT: You know, I'm really not an outdoorsy person. And I

9   don't like the cold. Snow does not impress me. And the

10   sounds of nature? Well, I trashed my nature sound

11   machine I got for Christmas last year. It was annoying.

12   NURSE: OK, then think of something else! Anything else! The

13   Grand Canyon, the Taj Mahal, the Egyptian pyramids, The

14   Great Wall of China ... whatever makes you feel calm and

15   peaceful!

16   PATIENT: How about Big Al's Burger Joint?

17   NURSE: Big Al's Burger Joint? You'd pick that over the Taj

18   Mahal?

19   PATIENT: Uh-huh. Have you ever had one of Big Al's burgers?

20   NURSE: I have not.

21   PATIENT: They are to die for. In fact, it will be my reward for

22   getting a shot today.

23   NURSE: That's a good idea. Because I'm sure you wouldn't

24   want one of the dinky little plastic toys we hand out to the

25   children. But a burger from Big Al's? Now that's a reward!

26   *(Smiles.)* I'll be right back.

27   PATENT: Wait!

28   NURSE: Yes?

29   PATIENT: Where are you going?

30   NURSE: To get something.

31   PATIENT: What?

32   NURSE: You know.

33   PATIENT: Wait!

34   NURSE: What?

35   PATIENT: Do you think you could show me how it's done first

1   **without actually doing it?**

2   **NURSE: You mean give you a pretend shot?**

3   **PATIENT: Yes. Please. I think it would help calm my fears.**

4   **NURSE: Well, all right. But then we're going to get this over**

5   **with. Agreed?**

6   **PATIENT: Agreed.**

7   **NURSE: So first I will take a cotton ball and rub a little alcohol**

8   **on your arm to clean the area so it doesn't get infected.**

9   **PATIENT: The area where you are going to jab me with the**

10   **needle?**

11   **NURSE: The area where I will give you a *quick stick* that will**

12   **last for half a millisecond.**

13   **PATIENT: That's a lie.**

14   **NURSE: Excuse me?**

15   **PATIENT: That's a lie that it'll only last for half a millisecond.**

16   **Do you know how long that really is?**

17   **NURSE: It's not long. I know that. Wow, you are difficult, aren't**

18   **you?**

19   **PATIENT: Well, a millisecond is one thousandth of a second. So**

20   **half of a millisecond is ... well ... one half of that. But if you**

21   **could make my shot last a nanosecond, that'd be great!**

22   **NURSE: Which is?**

23   **PATIENT: One billionth of a second.**

24   **NURSE: I don't know why we are having this conversation.**

25   **Look, it's not going to last that long, OK? So close your eyes**

26   **and think about Big Al's burgers and I'll be back in a blink**

27   **of an eye.**

28   **PATIENT: That's a lie, too.**

29   **NURSE: What's a lie?**

30   **PATIENT: That you'll be back in the blink of an eye. Look.**

31   **(*Blinks.*) I already blinked five times and you couldn't get**

32   **out the door by then. So maybe you should say you'll be**

33   **back in a hundred blinks of an eye.**

34   **NURSE: I'll be back!**

35   **PATIENT: Wait! Please! Wait!**

1   NURSE: *What?*

2   PATIENT: We didn't finish my pretend shot. I really need it to

3   prepare myself mentally for what's about to happen.

4   Please!

5   NURSE: *(Frustrated and angry)* I rub the alcohol on your arm

6   like this *(Rubs quick and hard)* to prevent germs from

7   entering your body!

8   PATIENT: Owwww! Not that hard, OK?

9   NURSE: And then while you are looking away ... Look away,

10   please! *(PATIENT looks away.)* And while you are imagining

11   yourself at Big Al's Hamburger Place —

12   PATIENT: It's Big Al's Hamburger *Joint.*

13   NURSE: And while you are imagining yourself at Big Al's

14   Hamburger Joint, I give you a shot! *(Pinches PATIENT.)*

15   PATIENT: *(Screams.)* **Owwww!** *(Almost crying)* Oh, my gosh! Oh,

16   my gosh!

17   NURSE: You can't do that! That was a pretend shot! You didn't

18   feel anything!

19   PATIENT: Yes I did! It felt like a real shot!

20   NURSE: You're insane! I'll be back.

21   PATIENT: No! Wait!

22   NURSE: I'll be back in fifty blinks of an eye ... or less! *(Steps*

23   *back.)*

24   PATIENT: No! No, wait! I'm not ready! Fifty blinks of an eye or

25   less? *(Blinks.)* One. *(Blinks.)* Two. *(Blinks.)* Three ... I can't

26   do this! Oh, my gosh, I can't do this! Big Al's burgers ... Big

27   Al's burgers ... No. It's not working! No, try! Big Al's

28   burgers. Big Al's burgers ... jalapeno's, onions, cheese ...

29   It's not working! ... No! But I have to do this! I have to! I am

30   not afraid! I am not afraid! I am not afraid! Oh, yes I am! I

31   am afraid! No! Big Al's burgers. Big Al's burgers. With

32   fries! And lots of ketchup. Where's the salt? I like salt. But

33   I hate shots! What if I faint? What if ... what if ... I die?

34   NURSE: Millisecond, nanosecond ... insane is what she is! I'd

35   almost like to jab this needle in her arm and give it a

1   couple of good twists! Sorry! My bad! Oh, did that hurt? It
2   did? Well, grow up! Shots hurt! Yes, I should jab her arm
3   so hard that she screams and runs off. *(Laughs.)* Then
4   there she'd be, running around the office with a needle
5   stuck in her arm! Too afraid to look at it and too afraid to
6   pull it out herself. So, I guess I will have to do the sweet
7   task of removing the needle from her arm. In one quick
8   motion? A millisecond? A nanosecond? Ha! I will twist it
9   around and around and give it another good jab ... that'll
10 teach her! *(Steps forward, hand in a fist.)* Are you ready?
11 PATIENT: No! No! I need a minute!
12 NURSE: Minute's up. I have other patients to attend to.
13 PATIENT: *(Moves away.)* I need to focus first.
14 NURSE: On Big Al's burgers?
15 PATIENT: No. That's not working for me anymore.
16 NURSE: You still have the puppy and kitty poster.
17 PATIENT: No, that's not working either.
18 NURSE: The ceiling? You could lie on the table and count the
19   squares on the ceiling.
20 PATIENT: Oh, I'm not lying down! No way am I lying down!
21 NURSE: *(Steps toward her.)* Then look away and take a deep
22   breath.
23 PATIENT: *(Steps away.)* Wait! Wait! I need to focus on
24   something.
25 NURSE: Close your eyes.
26 PATIENT: No! I'm afraid of the dark! I'd rather look at
27   something.
28 NURSE: I could turn the faucet on and you could watch the
29   water drip.
30 PATIENT: No! I hate the water! Remember? The ocean! The
31   sharks!
32 NURSE: There are no sharks in the sink.
33 PATIENT: Something else. Something else ...
34 NURSE: Would you like to hold a tongue depressor?
35 PATIENT: Why would I want to hold a tongue depressor?

1   NURSE: So that you could pretend you're holding a person's
2   hand.
3   PATIENT: No, I don't want to do that! But what I want to do is
4   leave this place! Leave this room! I feel like I've been in
5   here forever!
6   NURSE: You have. And you could have left so long ago. So if
7   you're ready ...
8   PATIENT: No! I'm not! I need to focus! I need to focus on
9   something!
10 NURSE: Focus on this being over. Focus on walking out to your
11   car.
12 PATIENT: Yes. Yes. I like that thought. I'm walking out of here.
13   Keys in my hand. I hear the beep as I unlock the car door ...
14 NURSE: *(Steps forward.)* Don't look ...
15 PATIENT: No! No! Wait!
16 NURSE: And as soon as I'm finished, you may leave.
17 PATIENT: First, tell me this: How many blinks is it going to
18   take?
19 NURSE: One ... maybe two.
20 PATIENT: Wait! I need a second! *(Begins doing jumping jacks.)*
21 NURSE: What are you doing?
22 PATIENT: This helps, OK?
23 NURSE: Jumping jacks help?
24 PATIENT: I feel in control when I move around! Like I'm alive!
25   Yes, I feel alive! *(Begins to jog in place.)* As if I'm going
26   somewhere! Far, far away!
27 NURSE: No, you're not! You're jogging in place in the doctor's
28   office.
29 PATIENT: But not in my mind! In my mind I'm at the
30   Comanche Trail Park. Jogging. Feeling the warm sun hit
31   my face. Wow! What a beautiful day!
32 NURSE: You have to watch out for snakes at the Comanche
33   Trail Park.
34 PATIENT: *(Stops jogging.)* What?
35 NURSE: At least this time of year. At least that's what I've heard.

1   That the snakes are very bad.

2 PATIENT: Why do you have to ruin everything?

3 NURSE: I'm just looking out for your health. That's funny, isn't

4   it? Because I am a nurse. And speaking of your health ...

5 PATIENT: *(Begins to jog again.)* On the track at the college! No

6   snakes there!

7 NURSE: Would you stop it!

8 PATIENT: Can't!

9 NURSE: Yes, you can!

10 PATIENT: Need to move! Need to feel alive! Need to keep

11   moving!

12 NURSE: I'll be back.

13 PATIENT: *(Stops jogging.)* You're leaving?

14 NURSE: Lunchtime. Need to eat. Need to feed my face.

15 PATIENT: Wait! I can do this! I want to do this! I want to get this

16   over with! For myself and for my health.

17 NURSE: Are you sure?

18 PATIENT: I'm sure. *(Holds out arm.)*

19 NURSE: Finally. *(Rubs alcohol on arm with cotton ball.)*

20 PATIENT: Big Al's burgers ... Big Al's burgers ... Big Al's burgers ...

21 NURSE: OK, we're finished.

22 PATIENT: Big Al's burgers ... Big Al's burgers ... Big Al's burgers ...

23 NURSE: I said we're finished.

24 PATIENT: We're finished?

25 NURSE: It's over.

26 PATIENT: It's over? But I didn't feel anything. Wow! That was

27   great! I didn't even feel any pain! After all that and shots

28   don't hurt after all!

29 NURSE: Look. *(As PATIENT looks, she jabs her hard with the shot,*

30   *laughing)* Sorry, but I lied! *(Laughing)* Feel this? *(Twists the*

31   *needle around and around)* Feel it? Feel it? Do you feel it?

32   OK, now we're finished! *(Smiles proudly.)*

33 PATIENT: *(Calmly)* Wow. That really wasn't bad at all. I mean, it

34   looked bad, but it wasn't bad. Maybe I felt a little pinch,

35   like you said I would, but really, there was nothing to it.

1   **Thanks!**
2   **NURSE: What do you mean it didn't hurt? It had to have hurt!**
3   **PATIENT: Guess I'm tougher than I thought. And now ...** *(Rubs*
4   *hands together)* **Big Al's burger, here I come!** *(She exits.)*
5
6
7
8
9
10
11
12
13
14
15
16
17
18
19
20
21
22
23
24
25
26
27
28
29
30
31
32
33
34
35

4. And the Winner Is ...

Cast: MARISSA and ANGELA
Setting: Beauty pageant

1 **MARISSA: Good luck.**

2 **ANGELA: Same to you.**

3 **MARISSA: You nervous?**

4 **ANGELA: A little. You?**

5 **MARISSA: A little. Do you suppose they'll ask us the same**
6 **questions?**

7 **ANGELA: Probably. I just hope it's not about world peace.**

8 **MARISSA: Me too. I hate that question.**

9 **ANGELA: Because the truth is, world peace is impossible.**

10 **MARISSA: Unless you created a human race who believed in**
11 **the same religion and political ideas.**

12 **ANGELA: Or who could agree to disagree.**

13 **MARISSA: I mean, can't we all just get along?**

14 **ANGELA: Lump it or leave it!**

15 **MARISSA: Isn't it *like* it or lump it?**

16 **ANGELA: I'm not sure.**

17 **MARISSA: What does that mean anyway? To lump it?**

18 **ANGELA: I guess it means to leave if you don't like it. Isn't that**
19 **right?**

20 **MARISSA: I guess so.**

21 **ANGELA: So back to the question about world peace.**

22 **MARISSA and ANGELA:** *(Look straight ahead and speak.)* **Yes, I**
23 **believe world peace is possible.**

24 **ANGELA: Peace between nations ...**

25 **MARISSA: Within our own country ...**

26 **ANGELA: And within our own cities ...**

1 MARISSA: And I believe ...
2 ANGELA: I believe ...
3 MARISSA: Peace begins with each individual ...
4 ANGELA: You and me.
5 MARISSA: *(Pauses and looks at ANGELA.)* Or is that you and I?
6 ANGELA: It's the same thing, isn't it?
7 MARISSA: I can't remember which is the proper saying. You
8   and me or you and I?
9 ANGELA: Well, I don't know. Which do you think sounds the
10   best?
11 MARISSA: You and me sounds best, but I have a feeling it's you
12   and I.
13 ANGELA: But hopefully no one will notice, right?
14 MARISSA: Hopefully.
15 ANGELA: *(Looks ahead and smiles.)* And if I'm crowned Miss
16   South Jackson Beauty Queen ...
17 MARISSA: *(Looks ahead and smiles.)* If I'm crowned Miss South
18   Jackson Beauty Queen ...
19 ANGELA: I will encourage all nations to unite ...
20 MARISSA: To come together to resolve all conflicts through
21   nonviolent means.
22 ANGELA: Peace and goodwill ...
23 MARISSA and ANGELA: Among all men. *(They smile.)*
24 MARISSA: Oh, and let's hope that they don't ask us about the
25   starving children in Africa.
26 ANGELA: Really! I mean, is a beauty pageant really the proper
27   place for such a topic? Doesn't it seem rather
28   inappropriate?
29 MARISSA: Especially when I've practically starved myself for
30   this pageant.
31 ANGELA: Me and you both.
32 MARISSA: Isn't that you and I?
33 ANGELA: You and I, me and you ... you know what I mean!
34 MARISSA and ANGELA: *(Look ahead and speak.)* Starving
35   children is a global crisis ...

1   ANGELA: A crisis that can't be ignored ...

2   MARISSA: A battle that must be won ...

3   ANGELA: And if I'm crowned Miss South Jackson Beauty

4   Queen ...

5   MARISSA: If I'm crowned Miss South Jackson Beauty Queen ...

6   ANGELA: I will volunteer my time to help those less fortunate ...

7   MARISSA: By working at the local food bank ...

8   ANGELA: And encourage donations to organizations that fight

9   childhood hunger ...

10 MARISSA: So that one day ...

11 ANGELA: One day ...

12 MARISSA and ANGELA: We will see the end of childhood

13   hunger.

14 ANGELA: Oh, and I hope they don't ask us about teen

15   pregnancies.

16 MARISSA: Protection, girls! Protection!

17 ANGELA: You know you can't say that if you want to win the

18   competition. Abstinence.

19 MARISSA: Abstinence, girls! Abstinence!

20 MARISSA and ANGELA: *(Look ahead and speak.)* Teen

21   pregnancy is a major issue facing our youth these days.

22 MARISSA: The statistics are alarming ...

23 ANGELA: I forgot the statistics.

24 MARISSA: Me too. So I'll just make something up. Sixty-two

25   percent of girls ...

26 ANGELA: Uh ... isn't that a bit high?

27 MARISSA: Then what is it?

28 ANGELA: I think it's thirty-four percent.

29 MARISSA: Are you sure?

30 ANGELA: Not sure, but I think ...

31 MARISSA: Well, it sounds good to me. *(Looks ahead and smiles.)*

32   Thirty-four percent of teen girls become pregnant ...

33 ANGELA: The highest teen pregnancy rate in the world ...

34 MARISSA: And teen mothers are less likely to complete high

35   school ...

1   **ANGELA: Or attend college ...**

2   **MARISSA: Which leads to lower paying jobs ...**

3   **MARISSA: Welfare ...**

4   **ANGELA: And feelings of shame and fear ...**

5   **MARISSA: And if I'm crowned Miss South Jackson Beauty**

6   **Queen ...**

7   **ANGELA: If I'm crowned Miss South Jackson Beauty Queen ...**

8   **MARISSA: I will promote more education to teens and parents ...**

9   **ANGELA: And encourage personal responsibility ...**

10   **MARISSA: And most of all ...**

11   **ANGELA: Most of all ...**

12   **MARISSA and ANGELA: I will encourage abstinence.** *(Pause as*

13   *they smile)*

14   **MARISSA: Oh, and please don't ask us about global warming.**

15   **Because what I want to say and must say are two different**

16   **things. "Global warming, you ask? How about this for an**

17   **answer? I could care less! Unless of course it affected me**

18   **winning the pageant."**

19   **MARISSA and ANGELA:** *(Look ahead and speak)* **Global warming**

20   **is a serious challenge that needs to be addressed ...**

21   **ANGELA: The health and economic well-being of future**

22   **generations must be protected ...**

23   **MARISSA: Heat waves ...**

24   **ANGELA: Melting glaciers ...**

25   **MARISSA: Rising sea levels ...**

26   **ANGELA: Changes in plants and animals ...**

27   **MARISSA: Downpours ...**

28   **ANGELA: And if I'm crowned Miss South Jackson Beauty**

29   **Queen ...**

30   **MARISSA: If I'm crowned Miss South Jackson Beauty Queen ...**

31   **ANGELA: I will promote greener choices ...**

32   **MARISSA: Go green!**

33   **ANGELA:** *(To MARISSA)* **That's my line!** *(Looks ahead.)* **Go green!**

34   **MARISSA: No, I'm using that! Go green!**

35   **ANGELA: Whatever!**

1   MARISSA: Whatever!

2   MARISSA and ANGELA: *(Look ahead and speak.)* And I will
3   promote practical steps to reduce greenhouse gas
4   emissions. *(They smile.)*

5   ANGELA: Oh, enough worrying about all the questions. We'll
6   deal with them as they come.

7   MARISSA: How much time do we have?

8   ANGELA: A couple more minutes I think.

9   MARISSA: They must have a lot of sponsors to thank.

10 ANGELA: And when that little red light goes on ...

11 MARISSA: The final ten contestants will march back out onto
12   that bright stage.

13 ANGELA: To face the judges.

14 MARISSA: As the MC begins the final round.

15 ANGELA: The questions.

16 MARISSA: Good luck.

17 ANGELA: Thanks. Same to you. Wow, I can feel my heart
18   beating.

19 MARISSA: And my feet are killing me. That last jaunt across the
20   stage put another blister on my foot.

21 ANGELA: *(Taking deep breaths)* Breathe in, breathe out.
22   Breathe in, breath out. You know, I'll be glad when all of
23   this is over.

24 MARISSA: Me too. *(Smiles.)* And then ... to bask in the glory ...

25 ANGELA: Or not.

26 MARISSA: Just consider yourself a winner.

27 ANGELA: I am, thank you.

28 MARISSA: Because being in the top ten ...

29 ANGELA: Is definitely an accomplishment to be proud of.

30 MARISSA: But when they crown me Miss South Jackson Beauty
31   Queen ...

32 ANGELA: You mean when they crown you runner-up ...

33 MARISSA: I will look into the camera ...

34 ANGELA: I will look into the camera ...

35 MARISSA: As tears stream down my face ...

1   ANGELA: With an expression of shock ... even though ...

2   MARISSA: Knowing the entire time ...

3   MARISSA and ANGELA: I'd be crowned Miss South Jackson

4   Beauty Queen!

5   ANGELA: Look, obviously we can't both win.

6   MARISSA: Obviously not. But I can tell you that the other

7   contestants don't stand a chance.

8   ANGELA: I'd agree with that statement. Julie lost points when

9   she wore her evening gown during the swimsuit session.

10 MARISSA: And Jackie giggled all the way through the initial

11   interview.

12 ANGELA: Monique forgot to spit her gum out.

13 MARISSA: And Francis forgot the words to her song.

14 ANGELA: What about Marcy? She didn't stay in sync with the

15   rest of us during the opening song and dance.

16 MARISSA: And Danielle couldn't complete one sentence

17   without saying, "ummmm, like" or "ummmm, well."

18 ANGELA: And did you see Hailey rush through her entrance

19   like it was a speedwalking contest?

20 MARISSA: Yeah. And what about when Katherine fell into the

21   pit during the second song and dance?

22 ANGELA: Which leaves you and me.

23 MARISSA: The only two contestants who stand a chance. *(As if*

24   *hearing the results)* Me? Me?

25 ANGELA: I won? I can't believe it!

26 MARISSA: I'm shaking! I'm so ...

27 ANGELA: Surprised doesn't even explain what I'm feeling!

28 MARISSA: I'm so honored!

29 ANGELA: I'm so grateful! Thank you!

30 MARISSA: Oh, thank you!

31 ANGELA: Thank you so much! *(Pause)*

32 MARISSA: There's the light. Come on! We have to go! *(MARISSA*

33   *and ANGELA step forward, each with huge smiles. As they*

34   *speak to the judges and each other, they continually smile.)*

35 ANGELA: Yes, I'm ready for my question. *(Pause)* What is the

1   **biggest challenge to young people today? Uh … can you**
2   **repeat the question?**
3   **MARISSA:** *(Under her breath)* **I didn't know they were going to**
4   **ask that question!**
5   **ANGELA: Me neither!**
6   **MARISSA: Then you better make up something good!**
7   **ANGELA:** *(Looking ahead)* **The biggest challenges to youth today**
8   **is … is …**
9   **MARISSA: You better think of something!**
10   **ANGELA: Is … is … abstinence! Abstinence is increasingly**
11   **difficult in a society that promotes sex in advertisements.**
12   **Encouraging promiscuity instead of what is now**
13   **considered old-fashioned values. And if I'm crowned Miss**
14   **South Jackson Beauty Queen, I will encourage teens to**
15   **focus on their values instead of letting themselves be**
16   **persuaded by the media.** *(Smiles.)*
17   **MARISSA: Wow. I can't believe you pulled that off.**
18   **ANGELA:** *(Talking through her smile)* **You're next.**
19   **MARISSA:** *(Looks ahead.)* **Yes, I'm ready.** *(Pause)* **What freedom**
20   **do I value the most? Life, liberty, or the pursuit of**
21   **happiness?**
22   **ANGELA: It's a trick question. Good luck.**
23   **MARISSA: I didn't prepare for this one.**
24   **ANGELA: So you're going to have to wing it.**
25   **MARISSA:** *(Looking ahead)* **Life, liberty, or the pursuit of**
26   **happiness?**
27   **ANGELA: The judges are waiting for your answer. Any day now!**
28   **MARISSA: The freedom I value the most is …**
29   **ANGELA: Remember, it's a trick question.**
30   **MARISSA: Is … is life! Because without life, I cannot achieve**
31   **liberty or the pursuit of happiness. And to live … to live is**
32   **… is … is to live!**
33   **ANGELA:** *(Snickers.)* **Great answer! To live is to live?**
34   **MARISSA: And if I'm crowned Miss South Jackson Beauty**
35   **Queen, I will … uh … I will live my life to the fullest as I**

1   **pursue life, liberty, and happiness!**

2 **ANGELA: You can go ahead and congratulate me now.**

3 **MARISSA:** *(Looks at Angela.)* **Shut up! I'd never heard of that**

4   **question before. It wasn't even listed as a possible**

5   **question on our information sheet.**

6 **ANGELA: Because they want to catch us off guard and see how**

7   **we answer. Not ask us a question that can be easily**

8   **answered or have been memorized.**

9 **MARISSA: So now we wait.**

10 **ANGELA: Wait for them to announce the winner.** *(Pause)* **I'm so**

11   **excited!**

12 **MARISSA: I'll be excited when I can go home and eat some**

13   **pasta and donuts. I'm starving.**

14 **ANGELA: I'll have to watch my weight after they announce me**

15   **the winner.**

16 **MARISSA: I'll be eating. Oh, I can't wait! I may sit in front of the**

17   **TV for three days and do nothing but eat.**

18 **ANGELA: As I take interviews, make appearances, have photo**

19   **shoots ...**

20 **MARISSA: Here it comes. And the winner is ...**

21 **ANGELA: And the winner is ... ? What?** *What?*

22 **MARISSA: You have to be a gracious loser, remember?**

23 **ANGELA: How could they pick you over me? You, with your "to**

24   **live is to live" answer? I don't understand this!**

25 **MARISSA:** *(Steps forward.)* **Thank you! Oh, thank you! What?**

26   **I'm the runner-up? Oh. I thought ...**

27 **ANGELA: Oh! Getting ahead of yourself, were you? Oh! Here it**

28   **comes. And the winner is ...** *(She steps forward.)* **Oh, thank**

29   **you! Thank you! Thank you! I'm so honored to be crowned**

30   **Miss South Jackson Beauty Queen!**

31

32

33

34

35

5. Dirty Laundry

Cast: CLAIRE and DR. FRYE
Setting: Therapist's office

1 CLAIRE: Doctor Frye, this is hard for me. I've known for a while
2   that I needed to talk to someone – a professional – but I
3   just couldn't bring myself to do it.
4 DR. FRYE: What finally gave you the courage?
5 CLAIRE: Realizing that I was desperate to live a normal life.
6 DR. FRYE: I see. So tell me, Claire, what prevents you from
7   living a normal life?
8 CLAIRE: Just say it?
9 DR. FRYE: Yes.
10 CLAIRE: OK. *(Deep breath)* It's my dirty laundry.
11 DR. FRYE: So, you have a secret that needs to be exposed?
12 CLAIRE: Yes.
13 DR. FRYE: Claire, you do realize that our conversations are
14   strictly confidential?
15 CLAIRE: Yes. Otherwise I wouldn't be here.
16 DR. FRYE: Good. And with that being understood, you can feel
17   secure that any and all things that you tell me will remain
18   in this office. Whatever it may be. Multiple affairs,
19   stealing from your workplace, being a closet alcoholic,
20   murder –
21 CLAIRE: Murder?!
22 DR. FRYE: I'm just saying that no matter what secrets you're
23   hiding, you are free to confess them here in my office. And
24   as I said, your confessions will stay in this room.
25 CLAIRE: Thank you. I've needed to do this for so long, Doctor
26   Frye. Face this ... oh ... *(Tears up.)* I'm sorry. May I have a
27   tissue?

1   DR. FRYE: Certainly. *(Hands her a tissue.)* **So let's continue. You**
2   **need to confess ... ?**
3   CLAIRE: Yes. My dirty laundry ...
4   DR. FRYE: Go on.
5   CLAIRE: It's just piling up everywhere!
6   DR. FRYE: I see. And it's affecting others?
7   CLAIRE: Well, no. I don't think it affects others.
8   DR. FRYE: But the guilt is getting to you?
9   CLAIRE: Mostly the stench.
10   DR. FRYE: I see. So what started this issue for you?
11   CLAIRE: Stuffing it under the bed.
12   DR. FRYE: Ignoring it?
13   CLAIRE: Exactly.
14   DR. FRYE: So we're clear about you attempting to stuff your
15   secrets and hide them?
16   CLAIRE: Yes.
17   DR. FRYE: All right. Then let's talk about the actual acts you
18   have engaged in.
19   CLAIRE: Do we have to go into the details?
20   DR. FRYE: I think it would be helpful. And prudent to your
21   recovery.
22   CLAIRE: All right. I'll try to be more specific with the details.
23   DR. FRYE: So tell me. What exactly have you done? What has
24   kept you awake at night? Caused you to feel overwhelmed
25   and ashamed?
26   CLAIRE: I told you. My dirty laundry.
27   DR. FRYE: Yes, yes, and now it's time to confess to your crimes.
28   Right here in the safety of my office.
29   CLAIRE: I'm trying, Doctor Frye.
30   DR. FRYE: I know it's hard allowing your shameful actions to
31   be expressed verbally. But Claire, it is the first step to
32   identifying your problems and understanding why you do
33   what you do.
34   CLAIRE: I know, Doctor Frye, but I don't know why I do what I
35   do!

1   **DR. FRYE:** I understand, Claire. But first you must be able to
2   tell someone – someone in a neutral position like myself
3   – about what you've done.
4   **CLAIRE:** *(Takes a deep breath.)* **OK.**
5   **DR. FRYE:** So tell me, when did this start?
6   **CLAIRE:** Probably in the fourth grade.
7   **DR. FRYE:** That young?
8   **CLAIRE:** Yes.
9   **DR. FRYE:** And you snuck liquor from your parents' bar when
10   they went to bed?
11   **CLAIRE:** No! I never did that!
12   **DR. FRYE:** Stole money from your mother's purse?
13   **CLAIRE:** No!
14   **DR. FRYE:** Then what did you do? Tell me, Claire.
15   **CLAIRE:** It was my mother. She was so mean.
16   **DR. FRYE:** Ah ... your mother.
17   **CLAIRE:** This is hard.
18   **DR. FRYE:** I know it's hard, Claire, but you can do this. So, your
19   mother was abusive ...
20   **CLAIRE:** It seemed that way to me.
21   **DR. FRYE:** Did she beat you?
22   **CLAIRE:** No, she didn't beat me. But she's the person who
23   caused me to do this horrible thing.
24   **DR FRYE:** Drugs.
25   **CLAIRE:** Drugs? No, I never did drugs!
26   **DR. FRYE:** Claire, we need to get to the bottom of this.
27   **CLAIRE:** The bottom of this is my dirty laundry!
28   **DR. FRYE:** Yes, and you need to air it out.
29   **CLAIRE:** No, I need to wash it!
30   **DR. FRYE:** Excuse me?
31   **CLAIRE:** I refuse to wash my dirty laundry! It started in fourth
32   grade.
33   **DR. FRYE:** You mean ... you're literally talking about dirty
34   laundry?
35   **CLAIRE:** Yes! It's what I've been trying to tell you all along! My

1   mother forced me to do my own laundry! And I hated it,

2   Doctor Frye! Absolutely hated it!

3 DR. FRYE: And you reached your boiling point and you did

4   something horrible, didn't you? Remember, Claire, this

5   conversation is strictly confidential.

6 CLAIRE: What are you suggesting, Doctor Frye? That I did

7   something horrendous to my own mother?

8 DR. FRYE: People reach their limits, Claire. Childhood abuse

9   and neglect sometimes don't rear their ugly heads until

10   years later.

11 CLAIRE: Well, I refused to visit her last Christmas.

12 DR. FRYE: I see. Then what?

13 CLAIRE: Then she insisted on coming over to my apartment.

14 DR. FRYE: So what happened?

15 CLAIRE: Well, she just showed up at my doorstep with an

16   armload of Christmas gifts. And that's when I lost it! I

17   mean, really lost it!

18 DR. FRYE: What did you do, Claire?

19 CLAIRE: I ... I ...

20 DR. FRYE: Tell me.

21 CLAIRE: I opened the door and I ...

22 DR. FRYE: Yes?

23 CLAIRE: I lied.

24 DR. FRYE: You lied?

25 CLAIRE: I told her she couldn't come in because I just had the

26   house fumigated and I didn't want the smell to knock her

27   over.

28 DR. FRYE: But there was more to it than that, correct?

29 CLAIRE: Yes. A lot more to it.

30 DR. FRYE: OK, let's take a step back to see if we can't figure out

31   what caused you to snap.

32 CLAIRE: *(Takes a deep breathe.)* OK.

33 DR. FRYE: You detest dirty laundry, correct?

34 CLAIRE: Yes. It has made me into this ... this horrible person.

35   *(Begins to cry.)* And I hate what I've become!

1   DR. FRYE: The abuse your mother inflicted on you is not your
2   fault, Claire.
3   CLAIRE: I'm not sure it was abusive, Doctor Frye.
4   DR. FRYE: Denial is often the first step to overcome.
5   CLAIRE: But my other friends had to do their own laundry and
6   they didn't grow up with the problems I have.
7   DR. FRYE: You cannot compare yourself to others, Claire. The
8   abuse was obviously more than you could handle. Which
9   in turn forced you to do things most people would never
10   dream of. But that does not mean it's your fault. So tell
11   me, do you hate your mother?
12 CLAIRE: Do I hate her? No, I don't think I hate her.
13 DR. FRYE: Let's be honest, Claire.
14 CLAIRE: But hate is such a strong word.
15 DR. FRYE: An abusive parent will cause their victims' thoughts
16   to become irrational. In turn, causing you to act out and
17   sometimes perform unmentionable acts. And I'm sure as
18   the ugly details emerge you will see for yourself that your
19   mother was abusive.
20 CLAIRE: I guess I should feel somewhat relieved then.
21   Knowing it's not all my fault.
22 DR. FRYE: Exactly. So let's talk about how you acted out as a
23   child. What did you do with your anger?
24 CLAIRE: I was rebellious.
25 DR. FRYE: Which caused you to ... ?
26 CLAIRE: Stuff the dirty laundry under my bed. Throw it in my
27   closets. Behind the dresser. Sometimes in the trash.
28 DR. FRYE: And later you ... ?
29 CLAIRE: Never changed. Now I have nothing to wear.
30 DR. FRYE: So out of your frustrations, you ... ?
31 CLAIRE: Feel alone. I'm unable to have friends over to my
32   apartment.
33 DR. FRYE: And you've become a recluse?
34 CLAIRE: Not exactly a recluse. I mean, I do go out occasionally.
35   But I could never have my friends or family come over.

1   DR. FRYE: Because of what you're hiding?

2   CLAIRE: Yes.

3   DR. FRYE: Let's talk about what you're hiding, Claire.

4   CLAIRE: Well, you know those big black trash bags?

5   DR. FRYE: You're hiding something in black trash bags?

6   CLAIRE: *(Upset)* Yes. I stuffed my ... my ... oh, this is hard!

7   DR. FRYE: What do you have stuffed in the black trash bags,

8   Claire?

9   CLAIRE: You know!

10 DR. FRYE: No. Tell me, Claire.

11 CLAIRE: I told you this was hard!

12 DR. FRYE: I know. But you need to go on.

13 CLAIRE: To me it's terrible. I don't want anyone knowing what

14   I've done.

15 DR. FRYE: Especially the police, correct?

16 CLAIRE: The police?

17 DR. FRYE: This is serious, isn't it?

18 CLAIRE: Yes, I think it's serious. That's why I'm here.

19 DR. FRYE: I think you might need an attorney.

20 CLAIRE: An attorney? How is an attorney going to help me?

21 DR. FRYE: Well, you may need representation. Should I contact

22   one for you?

23 CLAIRE: I need an attorney for my dirty laundry?

24 DR. FRYE: Yes, I'm afraid you do.

25 CLAIRE: But ... shouldn't you just encourage me to work

26   through my issues? Get over my anger and learn to wash

27   my clothes?

28 DR. FRYE: So you'll remove the blood? The evidence?

29 CLAIRE: The blood, the grape juice stains, the barbeque sauce

30   that sometimes dribbles on my pants when I eat at Jack

31   Jordan's Barbeque Shack ...

32 DR. FRYE: Let's go back to your mother ...

33 CLAIRE: Do we have to?

34 DR. FRYE: I think we should. An abusive parent can be the start

35   of a horrid and uncontrollable life. And that's what I'm

1   looking at right here. The result of parenting gone wrong.

2   Oh, I can see the subpoenas coming my way.

3   CLAIRE: Subpoenas?

4   DR. FRYE: They'll want me to testify.

5   CLAIRE: About me?

6   DR. FRYE: About what you've confessed. Well, what you're

7   about to confess.

8   CLAIRE: But you said our conversations were confidential!

9   DR. FRYE: Yes, but if I get subpoenaed by the court ...

10   CLAIRE: The court?

11   DR. FRYE: Oh, and the media will have a field day with this.

12   They will probably be swarming my office in no time. But

13   ... a little excitement around here ... I don't know. It could

14   be fun.

15   CLAIRE: The media?

16   DR. FRYE: Yes. All the major networks will want to interview

17   me. I may need an attorney as well.

18   CLAIRE: Over my dirty laundry?!

19   DR. FRYE: Over me cracking this case. When you confess to the

20   contents of those black trash bags.

21   CLAIRE: I didn't confess to anything criminal!

22   DR. FRYE: No, but we know where the evidence is now. I even

23   have your confession — well, somewhat of a confession —

24   recorded.

25   CLAIRE: You recorded our conversation?

26   DR. FRYE: I always record the conversations with my clients.

27   And this one ... who would have thought? Would you

28   excuse me for a moment?

29   CLAIRE: Where are you going?

30   DR. FRYE: Sit still. I just have to make a phone call.

31   CLAIRE: Who are you calling? The police?

32   DR. FRYE: And I'm going to lock the door behind me. But that's

33   just for your safety.

34   CLAIRE: You're calling the police over my dirty laundry? Like

35   they're going to arrest me over that?

1   **DR. FRYE:** And listen, I will visit you in jail.

2   **CLAIRE:** I'm going to jail over my dirty laundry?! Is it like a
3   health hazard or something?

4   **DR. FRYE:** How many trash bags are there, Claire?

5   **CLAIRE:** I don't know. I lost count. Hundreds, I suppose. All
6   stuffed full of —

7   **DR. FRYE:** Oh, those poor people!

8   **CLAIRE:** What poor people? No one comes to my apartment!

9   **DR. FRYE:** Don't you mean that no one *leaves* your apartment?

10 **CLAIRE:** No! I didn't say that.

11 **DR. FRYE:** Oh, the stench must be horrendous.

12 **CLAIRE:** I told you it was!

13 **DR. FRYE:** If you would just excuse me ...

14 **CLAIRE:** Do you want to see a picture?

15 **DR. FRYE:** You brought a picture of the evidence?

16 **CLAIRE:** Yes. I didn't think you'd believe me.

17 **DR. FRYE:** Yes, let me see. It might be difficult to look at, but
18   the police will need it for their case against you.

19 **CLAIRE:** I still don't understand why you are bringing the
20   police into it.

21 **DR. FRYE:** It's my civic duty.

22 **CLAIRE:** Your duty? That makes no sense to me! But here!
23   Look!

24 **DR. FRYE:** *(Pause as she looks at the photo)* But ... this is laundry!

25 **CLAIRE:** I know! It's my dirty laundry! I've been talking to you
26   about it, remember? How I've refused to wash my clothes
27   because my mother forced me to do it as a kid.

28 **DR. FRYE:** This is your dirty laundry?

29 **CLAIRE:** Yes!

30 **DR. FRYE:** Trash bags full of dirty laundry? Not trash bags of
31   dead people?

32 **CLAIRE:** Dead people? Where did you get that idea?

33 **DR. FRYE:** I don't know. I just thought ...

34 **CLAIRE:** So, are you still calling the police? So they can rush
35   over to my apartment and discover health code violations?

1   Thanks a lot, Doctor Frye! Thanks for helping me face my
2   issues and finding a way to deal with it!
3   DR. FRYE: You want me to help you deal with this?
4   CLAIRE: That's why I came to your office!
5   DR. FRYE: Well, let me give you a little advice, Claire.
6   CLAIRE: Finally!
7   DR. FRYE: Here's what I would suggest you do.
8   CLAIRE: Yes?
9   DR. FRYE: Wash your stinkin' laundry! That's my advice! Wash
10   it, dry it, and hang it up! And you know what else?
11   CLAIRE: What?
12   DR. FRYE: You might want to iron it, too!
13
14
15
16
17
18
19
20
21
22
23
24
25
26
27
28
29
30
31
32
33
34
35

6. Marriage Phobia

Cast: OLIVIA and EMMA
Setting: Olivia's kitchen

1   OLIVIA: So tell me! What did you say?

2   EMMA: It's not good.

3   OLIVIA: Tell me!

4   EMMA: It's not exactly what I said, but what I did.

5   OLIVIA: What did you do?

6   EMMA: I covered my ears and ran out screaming.

7   OLIVIA: You didn't!

8   EMMA: I did.

9   OLIVIA: Did he chase you?

10 EMMA: He tried, but he couldn't catch up. Later I sent him a
11   text and told him I needed to think.

12 OLIVIA: I bet his feelings were hurt.

13 EMMA: They'll be more hurt when I tell him no.

14 OLIVIA: Emma, you and Jared have been dating for five years,
15   so a marriage proposal would seem like the obvious next
16   step.

17 EMMA: But I don't want to marry Jared!

18 OLIVIA: Why not?

19 EMMA: Do you want a list?

20 OLIVIA: Just give me the top reason.

21 EMMA: Because he irritates me like no other!

22 OLIVIA: Be a little more specific.

23 EMMA: Nose hairs.

24 OLIVIA: What?

25 EMMA: Nose hairs! Curly black bristles hanging out of his nose!
26   It's not attractive, Olivia!

48

1   **OLIVIA: What else?**

2   **EMMA: What else?** Well, listening to his annoying laugh.

3   Because when Jared laughs it takes the fun out of

4   whatever was humorous. Talk about killing the moment!

5   **OLIVIA: Anything else?**

6   **EMMA:** There are so many irritants about Jared that it'd take

7   forever to tell them all to you.

8   **OLIVIA: Then why did you date him, Emma?**

9   **EMMA:** I don't know. It's not like I had many other options out

10   there. And it was nice having someone to do things with.

11   Like going to movies, going out to eat ...

12   **OLIVIA: So Jared was more like a friend than anything else?**

13   **EMMA:** I'm afraid so. And now he's messed it all up by

14   proposing.

15   **OLIVIA: Well, maybe you could explain to Jared that you like**

16   **the way things are now.**

17   **EMMA:** I've told him that all along, Olivia. But he's tired of our

18   relationship going nowhere. I should have known this

19   was going to happen because he's been hinting at this

20   marriage proposal for a good year.

21   **OLIVIA: He probably wants kids, too.**

22   **EMMA:** Yes, he does. He talks about it all the time. And can you

23   imagine me having kids?

24   **OLIVIA: Not really.**

25   **EMMA:** Me, stuck at home with little bald headed babies with

26   hairy noses.

27   **OLIVIA: So it's a definite no?**

28   **EMMA:** There's no way in a million years I'd marry Jared.

29   **OLIVIA: So now you have to break it to him.**

30   **EMMA:** I thought I did that by running out the door screaming

31   with my hands over my ears. But for some reason, he's

32   expecting me to come to my senses and run back into his

33   arms with a great big yes. He called earlier and

34   apologized.

35   **OLIVIA: He apologized?**

1   **EMMA:** Yes. For proposing at Walmart.

2   **OLIVIA:** Walmart?

3   **EMMA:** Next to the frozen pizzas. He said he realized he was

4   not being very romantic or thoughtful and it must have

5   caught me off guard and he understands why I would run

6   away like I did. He wants to take me to a nice Italian

7   restaurant tonight.

8   **OLIVIA:** For a redo?

9   **EMMA:** I'm afraid so. And that's why I need your help.

10   **OLIVIA:** What can I do?

11   **EMMA:** Help me figure out a way to tell Jared no without

12   hurting his feelings.

13   **OLIVIA:** Emma, I'm not sure that's possible. After five years of

14   dating, he's going to be hurt when you turn down his

15   proposal. He'll probably be crushed.

16   **EMMA:** I don't want to crush Jared. But I don't want to marry

17   him either. Olivia, help me think of a good excuse why I

18   can't marry him. Please!

19   **OLIVIA:** OK, OK. Let's see … I know. You have a life-threatening

20   illness.

21   **EMMA:** And I don't want to marry him because I'm dying?

22   **OLIVIA:** Sure! Why not?

23   **EMMA:** Because Jared would insist on taking care of me as I

24   wither away. And I don't want to pretend I'm dying. That

25   would be exhausting. And then when I don't die, then

26   what?

27   **OLIVIA:** OK, so you're not dying, but you have a disease.

28   **EMMA:** Olivia!

29   **OLIVIA:** A very rare disease …

30   **EMMA:** I can't wait to hear this.

31   **OLIVIA:** Which will slowly cause your skin to rot away …

32   **EMMA:** No!

33   **OLIVIA:** And you don't want him seeing you like that.

34   **EMMA:** No! That's ridiculous. And he'd never believe that.

35   **OLIVIA:** Then how about a mental disorder?

1 EMMA: As if I'm a wacko?
2 OLIVIA: Which is controlled by medication, but sometimes you
3   have breakthrough episodes.
4 EMMA: He might believe that.
5 OLIVIA: And you mainly struggle with phobias.
6 EMMA: Like phobias of snakes or spiders?
7 OLIVIA: Yes, and others. Many others.
8 EMMA: He knows I have a fear of heights.
9 OLIVIA: That could be one.
10 EMMA: And tomatoes.
11 OLIVIA: You're afraid of tomatoes?
12 EMMA: Yes. My mother made me eat them as a child and now
13   they scare me.
14 OLIVIA: Good, good. I mean, not good you were forced to eat
15   tomatoes, but good that Jared will believe you have phobia
16   issues. And your main fear, your main phobia ...
17 EMMA: Is ... ?
18 OLIVIA: Marriage.
19 EMMA: Of course! That's perfect!
20 OLIVIA: So, tell Jared that your marriage phobia gives you a
21   feeling of extreme anxiety. And when you're exposed to
22   your fear ...
23 EMMA: A marriage proposal ...
24 OLIVIA: You act irrationally.
25 EMMA: Which obviously I did when I ran out of Walmart
26   screaming like a crazy person.
27 OLIVIA: Exactly. And Jared needs to understand that you must
28   do everything you can to avoid that situation again.
29   Because your fears trigger an extreme physical reaction.
30   Shortness of breath, sweating excessively, dizziness,
31   shaking, trembling ...
32 EMMA: And Jared wouldn't want to be the cause of me falling
33   apart.
34 OLIVIA: Unless ...
35 EMMA: Unless what?

1   OLIVIA: Unless he wants to help you work through your fears.

2   EMMA: I didn't think about that.

3   OLIVIA: But maybe if he sees how terrible it is for you he won't

4   be able to cope with being the cause of your meltdown.

5   EMMA: How could he if he really loves me?

6   OLIVIA: So you have to make it as believable as possible. He

7   needs to see the ugly picture for himself.

8   EMMA: Then maybe I should practice.

9   OLIVIA: Good idea.

10 EMMA: OK, ask me to marry you.

11 OLIVIA: OK. *(Takes her hand.)* Emma, will you marry me?

12 EMMA: *(Puts her hands over her ears and screams.)* No! No! No!

13   Air! Air! Air! I can't breathe! I need air! I need air!

14 OLIVIA: That was OK, but why don't you go into a complete

15   panic attack so you're sure that Jared believes you.

16 EMMA: I thought I just did.

17 OLIVIA: No, you can make it much worse than that.

18 EMMA: OK. I'll try.

19 OLIVIA: Let's do this again. *(Gets on one knee and takes her*

20   hand.)*

21 EMMA: *(Laughs.)* He's not going to get down on one knee.

22 OLIVIA: How do you know?

23 EMMA: Because he popped the question at Walmart. Jared is

24   not that romantic.

25 OLIVIA: He's taking you to a nice restaurant tonight. So he's

26   probably planning it all out as we speak. Even getting

27   down on one knee.

28 EMMA: Well, maybe.

29 OLIVIA: *(Still on one knee)* So I take out a small box ...

30 EMMA: *(Screams and covers ears with hands.)* No, no, no, no, no,

31   no! I can't breathe! I need air! I need air! Someone get me

32   a paper sack! I can't breathe!

33 OLIVIA: *(Taps her on the arm.)* Emma ...

34 EMMA: Was that good?

35 OLIVIA: It was OK, but you went into your panic attack before I

1   even proposed.

2 **EMMA:** Oh.

3 **OLIVIA:** Why don't we try something else?

4 **EMMA:** What?

5 **OLIVIA:** You be Jared and I'll be you. That way you can see it
6   from his perspective. As to what looks believable or not.

7 **EMMA:** Oh, OK. That's a good idea.

8 **OLIVIA:** So I'm you ...

9 **EMMA:** And I'm Jared. *(Takes OLIVIA's hand, in a deep voice)*
10   Emma, will you marry me?

11 **OLIVIA:** What did you say?!

12 **EMMA:** I said ...

13 **OLIVIA:** You said marriage?! Marriage?! *(Gasps for air.)* Oh! I
14   can't breathe! I can't breathe! Air! Air! I have to get out of
15   here! I have to get out of here! I can't breathe! Someone get
16   me out of here! *(Shaking)* I'm cold! So cold! I can't breathe!
17   Air! Air!

18 **EMMA:** *(Laughing)* I'm sorry! I don't mean to be laughing, but
19   that was funny.

20 **OLIVIA:** Emma!

21 **EMMA:** I'm sorry!

22 **OLIVIA:** OK, forget this reverse role playing. We're going back
23   to me being Jared and you being you because you've got to
24   get this figured out before dinner tonight.

25 **EMMA:** I know. You're right.

26 **OLIVIA:** I'm Jared and you're you. We're sitting at a nice Italian
27   restaurant and I pull out this small box and then I say,
28   "Emma, will you marry me?" *(Silence)* You're supposed to
29   go into your panic mode now. Hello?

30 **EMMA:** I know, but I was thinking.

31 **OLIVIA:** I've given you enough time to think, Emma. I need an
32   answer.

33 **EMMA:** I would, Jared, but ...

34 **OLIVIA:** But what? You're afraid of marriage?

35 **EMMA:** To you.

1 OLIVIA: What?
2 EMMA: I'm afraid to marry you, Jared.
3 OLIVIA: What do you mean you're afraid to marry me? Do I
4   make you feel like you're about to have a panic attack? To
5   the point you can't think or breathe and you want to run
6   out of this restaurant screaming?
7 EMMA: Jared, it's your hairy nose.
8 OLIVIA: What?
9 EMMA: If you could just trim them or pull them ... and while
10   we're on this subject, it's also your ears.
11 OLIVIA: My ears?
12 EMMA: Yes. You have these black curly hairs in your ears and I
13   find them quite disgusting. If you could pull them out, or
14   shave them, or have electrolysis done, I don't know. Maybe
15   I would feel different ...
16 OLIVIA: You're turned off by my hairy nose and ears?
17 EMMA: And there's something else.
18 OLIVIA: What?
19 EMMA: It's what you do after dinner when we're at a
20   restaurant.
21 OLIVIA: What?
22 EMMA: Floss your teeth with the little pink artificial sugar
23   packages, and then replace them in the holder for the
24   next customer.
25 OLIVIA: That bothers you?
26 EMMA: Yes that bothers me, Jared! You bother me. And there's
27   something else.
28 OLIVIA: There's more?
29 EMMA: Your laugh.
30 OLIVIA: My laugh?
31 EMMA: Have you ever heard yourself laugh, Jared?
32 OLIVIA: Well, yes. Of course I have.
33 EMMA: Well, I never want to hear you laugh again, Jared.
34   Because you sound like this. *(Imitates.)*
35 OLIVIA: But I love you, Emma.

1   EMMA: I'm sorry, Jared.

2   OLIVIA: So it's a no?

3   EMMA: And there's one more thing.

4   OLIVIA: What?

5   EMMA: I have a phobia.

6   OLIVIA: What kind of phobia?

7   EMMA: It's a marriage phobia.

8   OLIVIA: Come on! That's just an excuse.

9   EMMA: No it's not. It's real.

10 OLIVIA: You're making this up.

11 EMMA: No I'm not.

12 OLIVIA: I need an answer, Emma. For the last time, will you

13   marry me?

14 EMMA: *(Puts hands over ears and screams.)* No! No! No! No! No!

15   *(Drops to the floor in the fetal position and rocks back and*

16   *forth.)* I hate marriage! I hate marriage! I hate marriage! I

17   need air! I can't breathe! I need air! I want my mommy!

18   Mommy! Mommy! Mommy!

19 OLIVIA: Hey, that's pretty convincing. I think that'll keep Jared

20   from asking you again after that performance. *(Pause)* OK,

21   you can get up now, Emma. Emma? Emma, you can get up

22   now. Emma? Are you acting or is this real? Emma? Wow. I

23   think you do have a marriage phobia. Jared will definitely

24   be scared away from this. Actually, I'm starting to get a

25   little scared. Emma?

26 EMMA: I want my mommy ...

27

28

29

30

31

32

33

34

35

7. The Tryouts

Cast: PAULA and DEBBIE
Setting: School gym

1   *(At rise, PAULA and DEBBIE are watching their daughters*
2   *try out for cheerleader.)*
3   **PAULA:** *(Begins clapping loudly.)* **That was wonderful, Brianna!**
4   **Wonderful!** *(Turns to DEBBIE.)* **Wasn't that wonderful? I**
5   **tell you, all those years of hard work have paid off! That**
6   **was wonderful, sweetheart! Wonderful!** *(Blows her a kiss.)*
7   **DEBBIE:** *(Perks up.)* **Oh, my daughter is next!** *(As she is*
8   *watching)* **Yes, that's right, Jasmine ... keep smiling.**
9   *(Smiling)* **Big smile for the judges. That's right.** *(Imitates*
10   *her daughter's hand movements as she watches the cheer.)*
11   **Go, go, go ... fight, fight, fight ... Win!**
12   **PAULA: How long has Jasmine been preparing for the tryouts?**
13   **DEBBIE: Since this summer.**
14   **PAULA: Brianna started in the crib.**
15   **DEBBIE: What? As a newborn?**
16   **PAULA: That's right. Every time I changed Brianna's diaper, we**
17   **worked on stretching and practicing cheers. Go Cobras,**
18   **go! Go Cobras, go! Brianna would coo and smile at me and**
19   **I knew right then she was destined to be a cheerleader.**
20   **DEBBIE:** *(Suddenly)* **Yes! A great finish! Did you see her go**
21   **down into the splits? Yes, Jasmine! That was wonderful!**
22   **Yes! Solid and in control. And she's still smiling.** *(Claps*
23   *loudly.)* **Good, Jasmine!**
24   **PAULA: And by the time Brianna could walk, she could do a**
25   **little cheer. I even had a little cheerleading outfit made for**
26   **her. And I got her these cute little pompoms. And as**

1   Brianna took her first little steps, pompoms in hand, we'd
2   yell, "Go Cobras, go! Go Cobras, go!" You know what her
3   first sentence was?
4 DEBBIE: What's that?
5 PAULA: "Go, fight, win!" Her very first sentence! Isn't that cute?
6   "Go, fight, win!"
7 DEBBIE: Yes, that's quite something all right. Well, now for the
8   hard part. Waiting on the results.
9 PAULA: Yeah. I wonder how long the judges will take?
10 DEBBIE: I don't know. Last year it was a good thirty minutes
11   before they announced the winners.
12 PAULA: I remember. I brought Brianna to the tryouts so she
13   could see what to expect this year. Actually, I've brought
14   her to the tryouts every year since she was two-years-old. I
15   wanted her to feel comfortable in the gym for when she
16   had her own big day.
17 DEBBIE: Did you hear that? The cheerleading sponsor just said
18   the judges are asking the girls to perform their routine
19   one more time.
20 PAULA: Probably because they're having a difficult time making
21   their decision. With only two spots open this year ...
22 DEBBIE: And eleven girls trying out for those two spots ...
23 PAULA: Yes, it will be a tough decision.
24 DEBBIE: I feel sorry for the nine girls who don't make it.
25 PAULA: Yes. And thank goodness Brianna can sit back and
26   relax. After she does her cheer again, that is. She has
27   nothing to worry about. Like I said, she's been cheering
28   since the crib.
29 DEBBIE: Oh, Jasmine is going first. *(Claps.)* Go, Jasmine! She's
30   smiling. Keep smiling! The judges like that.
31 PAULA: And looks are important, too, you know. Brianna has
32   been tanning all winter. See how beautiful her skin looks?
33   I also had her teeth whitened. And if you ask me, she looks
34   like a California beauty queen.
35 DEBBIE: You can do this, baby! *(Hands on hips as she mimics*

1   *her daughter)* **Red hot, our team is red hot.** *(Throws her*
2   *arm out in front of PAULA.)*
3 **PAULA: Hey, watch it!**
4 **DEBBIE:** *(Arm movements)* **Red, red hot —**
5 **PAULA: Watch it!**
6 **DEBBIE: Once we start, we can't be stopped!** *(Attempts to do the*
7   *splits, then struggles to get up.)* **Oh, I forgot I couldn't do**
8   **that.**
9 **PAULA: That wasn't too bad. Your daughter, that is.**
10 **DEBBIE: Thank you. I think she's wonderful!**
11 **PAULA: Does Jasmine take lessons?**
12 **DEBBIE: Yes, from a college student down the street.**
13 **PAULA: How long has she been in lessons?**
14 **DEBBIE: Just this past year. Personally, I don't believe in**
15   **starting them out too young. You can damage their little**
16   **bodies if you push them before they're ready.**
17 **PAULA: Well, I disagree. From the crib to the football field at**
18   **our house. And oh, to be the envy of every girl. And**
19   **Brianna is such a natural. I remember one day when I was**
20   **changing her diaper, she kicked her little legs to the**
21   **rhythm of a new cheer I was teaching her.**
22 **DEBBIE: Are you serious?**
23 **PAULA: It's true! And when Brianna was three, I found her**
24   **teaching our dog a cheer she'd made up all by herself. Now**
25   **granted, it was a doggie cheer, with little barks in it, but it**
26   **was adorable. Go, arf, arf! Go, arf, arf! Oh, Brianna is next!**
27   *(Watches intently as she mimes the cheer.)* **Come on**
28   **everybody, stand up and clap your hands!** *(Claps.)* **Clap**
29   **your hands to the winning beat. Yell real loud and stomp**
30   **your feet.** *(Stomps her feet.)*
31 **DEBBIE: Ouch! That was my foot you just stomped on!**
32 **PAULA: Show them that we've got the spirit. Yell real loud and**
33   **let them hear it. Victory is ours, and ours to keep. Victory**
34   **is ours, we can't be beat!**
35 **DEBBIE: Not bad.**

1 PAULA: *(Claps loudly.)* **Wonderful! Wonderful! Wonderful!**

2 DEBBIE: **Now for the waiting.**

3 PAULA: *(Gives DEBBIE a hug.)* **I'm so excited! Aren't you excited?**

4 **Oh, Brianna has wanted this since she was a baby!**

5 DEBBIE: **I doubt your daughter knew what she wanted when**

6 **she was a baby. Other than needing milk and a diaper**

7 **change.**

8 PAULA: **No, it's true! It's like the moment Brianna began to cry,**

9 **she was saying to me, "Mommy, I want to be a cheerleader**

10 **when I grow up."**

11 DEBBIE: *(Laughs.)* **She didn't say that!**

12 PAULA: **Not the actual words, but her little cries told me that.**

13 *(Makes little crying sounds.)* **Mommy, I want to be a**

14 **cheerleader when I grow up.**

15 DEBBIE: **Well, with Jasmine, I simply asked her what activities**

16 **she'd like to participate in and gave her several options.**

17 **Like soccer, where you kick this stupid ball across the**

18 **field, music lessons where I'm going to constantly nag at**

19 **you to practice, or cheerleading where you get to wear**

20 **these cute little outfits and everyone loves you and wants**

21 **to be you. And believe it or not, she made her own decision**

22 **to become a cheerleader.**

23 PAULA: *(Hollers toward the judges.)* **Give us the results already!**

24 DEBBIE: **The girls look nervous, don't they?**

25 PAULA: **Most of them do. I think Brianna looks fairly calm.**

26 DEBBIE: **I bet the six returning girls are anxious to find out**

27 **who the two new girls are that will be joining them.**

28 PAULA: **I'm sure. And yes, I do feel sorry for the nine girls who**

29 **don't get chosen. I bet there will be a lot of tears and**

30 **heartaches here shortly.**

31 DEBBIE: **I'm afraid you're right.**

32 PAULA: *(Begins waving and hollering.)* **Brianna!** *(Gives her a*

33 *thumbs-up.)* **We're going to celebrate tonight!**

34 DEBBIE: **Or not.** *(PAULA gives her a look.)* **Jasmine, you did**

35 **marvelous, sweetheart!**

1   PAULA: Actually, we started celebrating last night.

2   DEBBIE: Before the results?

3   PAULA: Of course. We didn't need the results to be confident in

4   Brianna being selected today. Besides, last week I watched

5   all the girls in their mock tryout and she was without a

6   doubt the best.

7   DEBBIE: Well, I'm not saying your daughter isn't good, but

8   unless you paid off the judges, you can't know for sure.

9   PAULA: Look, it's based on athletic ability and confidence,

10   correct?

11   DEBBIE: And enthusiasm.

12   PAULA: And looks play a part as well.

13   DEBBIE: True.

14   PAULA: And Brianna has all of those qualities. Even you have to

15   admit that.

16   DEBBIE: What I have to admit is that Jasmine stands as good a

17   chance as your daughter or anyone else for that matter.

18   PAULA: But you realize that Brianna is years ahead of all these

19   other so-called wannabes.

20   DEBBIE: Wannabes?

21   PAULA: I'm sorry, but it's just so obvious to me. She stands out

22   and stands alone. They should choose one girl instead of

23   two and that should be my Brianna.

24   DEBBIE: Wow. The tears may not be confined to just the

25   students. Sounds like a mother could have a complete

26   meltdown.

27   PAULA: Oh, I'm so excited! Aren't you?

28   DEBBIE: Looks like the judges are tallying up the scores.

29   PAULA: Yes. Announcements will be coming soon. And not

30   soon enough. My sister Jonnie is setting up for the party as

31   we speak.

32   DEBBIE: What party?

33   PAULA: The celebration party. We reserved a room at the

34   country club. The tables are lined with confetti and mini

35   megaphones. Then I had this huge chocolate cake made

1   that says, "Brianna, Cheerleader."

2 DEBBIE: And what will you do if she loses?

3 PAULA: Oh, she won't lose, silly. And listen, you and your
4   daughter Jasmine are invited to the party. It might help
5   lift her spirits.

6 DEBBIE: Or she can be there to console your daughter and
7   keep her occupied while you scrape the word *Cheerleader*
8   off the cake.

9 PAULA: Why you ... Oh, look! The judge on the end is handing
10   the results to Mrs. Watters.

11 DEBBIE: Oh, this is it! *(Grabs PAULA's hand for support.)* Did you
12   hear that? They did have a difficult time with the decision
13   because all the girls were so good.

14 PAULA: And they wish they could take everyone ...

15 DEBBIE: But only two girls are to be chosen.

16 PAULA: Which will be Brianna and ... and ... What was that?
17   What did Mrs. Watters just say?

18 DEBBIE: So they said, "Why not?"

19 PAULA: Why not what?

20 DEBBIE: I don't know. I don't understand. Why are all the girls
21   jumping up and down and screaming?

22 PAULA: What? They're taking everyone?

23 DEBBIE: Everyone made it? All eleven girls?

24 PAULA: That's not fair!

25 DEBBIE: All eleven made it? But I don't understand!

26 PAULA: Those other girls don't deserve to be on a team with
27   Brianna!

28 DEBBIE: But isn't that too many cheerleaders? With six
29   returning girls and eleven trying out ...

30 PAULA: *(Screams.)* That's seventeen cheerleaders, judge!
31   Where's the competition?

32 DEBBIE: Obviously not here.

33 PAULA: No! This is not right! Brianna has been preparing for
34   this day since she was a newborn! She was ready to be
35   chosen as one of the best in this competition. But this ... ?

1   Taking all eleven girls?

2   DEBBIE: And I volunteered to help with the sixth grade dance

3   and graduation next year because I was certain Jasmine

4   would be a standout at school.

5   PAULA: Who ever heard of every girl making it?

6   DEBBIE: It's outrageous, that's what it is!

7   PAULA: And do you know what this means?

8   DEBBIE: What?

9   PAULA: Besides Brianna not standing out as one of the most

10   talented and popular girls, it means that there will be

11   seventeen — pay attention — seventeen cheerleaders to

12   cheer for the Cobras this year.

13 DEBBIE: Whoever heard of such a thing?

14 PAULA: And my Brianna was all prepared to hold her head up

15   and walk down the halls knowing she was better than

16   everyone else!

17 DEBBIE: And Jasmine has been working so hard for this! For

18   what? To be clumped together with the good, bad, and

19   mediocre?

20 PAULA: And to think, Brianna has been practicing for this day

21   since she was in her crib! *(Screams toward the judges.)* And

22   for this? *(Screams.)* For this? What kind of judges are you?

23 DEBBIE: Yeah, and what kind of school lets every fifth grader

24   who tries out for cheerleader make it?

25 PAULA: Oh! I just want to protest! Right here and right now!

26   How dare they do this to keep from hurting the other

27   girls' feelings? Who cares about all their feelings? We just

28   wanted the two best girls to win. *(Yells.)* Just pick the two

29   best girls, judge!

30 DEBBIE: Look at all the girls congratulating each other.

31   Hugging, laughing ... How can they be so happy?

32 PAULA: Brianna should be furious! She should throw her

33   pompoms down on the gym floor and stomp out!

34 DEBBIE: Look, she's hugging my daughter.

35 PAULA: *(Yells.)* Brianna, stop it!

1   DEBBIE: And now they are all giving each other high fives.

2   PAULA: You know what? I think I'm going to go and give Mrs.

3   Watters a piece of my mind! How dare she allow them to

4   pick all eleven girls! Since Brianna was a day old we've

5   been preparing to be a sixth grade Cobra cheerleader!

6   DEBBIE: I'm coming with you! And I'm going to find out why

7   Jasmine is so happy. I'm going to put a stop to this!

8   PAULA: I say we band together and insist they kick nine of

9   those girls off the team!

10   DEBBIE: I'm with you! Let's go! *(They give each other a high five*

11   *and exit.)*

12

13

14

15

16

17

18

19

20

21

22

23

24

25

26

27

28

29

30

31

32

33

34

35

8. Fired

Cast: LISA and JOLENE
Setting: Lisa's office at *The Rising Star News*

1   JOLENE: What did you want to see me about?

2   LISA: Jolene, I have something to discuss with you.

3   JOLENE: You read my story on sunglasses for dogs?

4   LISA: What? Sunglasses for dogs?

5   JOLENE: Yes. It protects your pet from harmful UV rays as well

6   　　　as being a fashion statement.

7   LISA: For dogs?

8   JOLENE: Yes. I read about it in a pet magazine and thought our

9   　　　readers would want to know more about this fascinating

10 　　　eyewear now available for dogs everywhere. And did you

11 　　　know that they also have designer sunglasses for our little

12 　　　pooches?

13 LISA: I did not.

14 JOLENE: Well, you should read my story, *Doggie Sunglasses,* by

15 　　　Jolene Matthews. And then I think you'll see that I'm

16 　　　ready to move up from the Lost and Found section to

17 　　　becoming a feature writer.

18 LISA: Jolene, this is not an easy thing for me to do.

19 JOLEEN: What's not easy for you? Oh, you didn't like my article,

20 　　　did you? OK, OK, if you'll just give me another shot at this.

21 　　　I have another story I'm working on titled, *Sending Your*

22 　　　*Pet Away with Dignity.* It's about buying caskets for your

23 　　　dead dog, or cat, or whatever you have. But I don't think

24 　　　small pet caskets are available for hamsters or gerbils. I'm

25 　　　not sure. But I can look into that.

26 LISA: Jolene, no —

1   JOLENE: Or I have this other story idea, *What You Should*
2   *Know About Breeding Dwarf Hamsters.* I think our
3   readers would be interested in that story, don't you?
4   LISA: Jolene, will you listen to me?
5   JOLENE: Yes, of course, but let me just say this. *Dogs and*
6   *Ringworm: What You Need to Know.* Now tell me you can't
7   say no to that story idea.
8   LISA: No!
9   JOLENE: *How to Care for Your Green Iguana?*
10   LISA: No!
11   JOLENE: Puppy potty training?
12   LISA: No!
13   JOLENE: Curing a dog's bad breath?
14   LISA: Jolene, we need to talk!
15   JOLENE: Last one. How about this idea for a story? *The Secrets*
16   *to Caring for Your Goldfish.*
17   LISA: Jolene ...
18   JOLENE: *(Smiling)* Yes?
19   LISA: I'm sorry, but I have to let you go.
20   JOLENE: What do you mean?
21   LISA: Jolene, you're fired.
22   JOLENE: You're firing me?
23   LISA: Yes, I'm afraid so.
24   JOLENE: Why?
25   LISA: Well, for one, it appears that you have a problem with
26   tardiness.
27   JOLENE: You're firing me because I was late for work?
28   LISA: Because you've been late for work every day.
29   JOLENE: But it's not without a good excuse!
30   LISA: Jolene, this is not high school.
31   JOLENE: I know that! Even though this is my first job since
32   graduating from high school ...
33   LISA: Well, hopefully you'll be more prompt at your next job.
34   JOLENE: But I love working at *The Rising Star News.* I even
35   envisioned myself moving up from the Lost and Found

1   section to writing a daily column.

2 LISA: Jolene, that's not the way it happens around here at *The*

3   *Rising Star.*

4 JOLENE: But the reason I was late —

5 LISA: Stop! At this point, it doesn't matter why you were late.

6 JOLENE: But listen! Please! The reason I was late is because I

7   was getting up at the crack of dawn to show my support

8   for the newspaper.

9 LISA: If you were getting up at the crack of dawn, then why

10   couldn't you be here on time?

11 JOLENE: Because I was working on the Lost and Found section.

12   Have you not noticed the increase of lost pets?

13 LISA: Actually yes. I have.

14 JOLENE: And have you not noticed how the ads in the Lost and

15   Found section have skyrocketed? It's practically become

16   the community's favorite section of the daily news.

17 LISA: Which shows you that we need the Lost and Found editor

18   to be on time.

19 JOLENE: I'm an editor? Wow. I never thought about it like that

20   before. The Lost and Found Editor. Wow. Oh, Lisa, you

21   can't fire me! Please! Let me explain what I've been doing!

22 LISA: I'm sorry, but we've already replaced you, Jolene.

23 JOLENE: With who?

24 LISA: Tori from the Household Goods section.

25 JOLENE: What? But that's not fair! Don't you realize that when

26   Tori takes over the Lost and Found section there will only

27   be a couple of lost pets a week? Not twenty or thirty like

28   we're having now!

29 LISA: And why is that, Jolene?

30 JOLENE: *(Looks around the office, then lowers her voice.)*

31   Because I've been helping my section grow. You know

32   what I mean?

33 LISA: No, I don't know what you mean, Jolene.

34 JOLENE: Face it, Lisa, until I came to work at *The Rising Star,*

35   the Lost and Found was slow, dull, and one of the

1   least-read sections.

2   LISA: Yes, I agree there has been a drastic increase in ads,
3   which is good for the paper, but what could you have
4   possibly done to increase that section?

5   JOLENE: *(Looks around the room again.)* Let me just say that the
6   reward money was a bonus, but that's not the reason I've
7   been doing it.

8   LISA: You've been out searching for the lost pets?

9   JOLENE: Oh, I've done more than that.

10   LISA: What do you mean?

11   JOLENE: Now let me start out by saying that those little lost
12   dogs and cats were never missing but for a day or two.

13   LISA: Because you found them?

14   JOLENE: Well, yes ... in a sense. In the morning at the crack of
15   dawn, they disappeared. Poor little things. Then the
16   following evening, they were found.

17   LISA: Oh, no! Tell me you didn't!

18   JOLENE: Oh, and if you could've seen the owners' faces when
19   their pets were returned home safely. The excitement, the
20   tears, and oh, the hugs for me. And yes, I usually received
21   reward money. I hated to take it, but whenever I turned it
22   down, the pet owners insisted I take the money. So what
23   could I say? Except thank you.

24   LISA: Jolene, how could you? What you've been doing is a
25   criminal offense. Ever heard of trespassing?

26   JOLENE: Oh, but I never trespassed! I mean, I never entered
27   anyone's backyard. Maybe ... somehow ... the gate just
28   happened to come ajar as I was standing there, and lo and
29   behold, I found a lost pet! But trespassing, no siree. So
30   anyway, being the kind and caring person that I am, I took
31   the animal home, cared for it, then returned it the
32   following day to its ecstatic owner.

33   LISA: So that's why you were late for work?

34   JOLENE: Yes. I was helping the paper increase its Lost and
35   Found ads.

1   LISA: This is unbelievable! I cannot believe you'd do something
2   like this! I should call the police and turn you in!
3   JOLENE: No, no, don't do that! Instead, why don't you give me a
4   promotion?
5   LISA: A promotion? Promote a thief? To what? The employment
6   section so you can make up bogus jobs and have our
7   readers send in their resumés to a blind box?
8   JOLENE: Hey, that's a great idea! Talk about improving your
9   readership with a huge amount of jobs listed every day!
10   Especially in today's economy!
11   LISA: Jolene, our newspaper prides itself on honesty and
12   clarity of facts, not lies and deception.
13   JOLENE: OK, OK, I know. So it was a bad idea. But you have to
14   admit it worked. So since Tori is taking over the Lost and
15   Found section now, what if you put me in charge of the
16   Dear Abby section?
17   LISA: You can't take over for a syndicated columnist! We'd get
18   sued if you altered one word in the Dear Abby section!
19   JOLENE: Then let's start a new column. *Dear Jolene.* It can be
20   our own local version of Dear Abby. And if the problems
21   are interesting enough, you know, we don't even have to
22   depend on our readers sending in their questions,
23   because I can do both. The complicated messy questions
24   and the no nonsensical answers.
25   LISA: OK, here's one for you. Let's say a teen girl writes in
26   saying she is upset because her parents are getting a
27   divorce. The letter would go something like this, "Dear
28   Jolene, I'm sixteen-years-old and I feel like my life is
29   coming to an end. My parents are getting a divorce. What
30   should I do? Please help me. Sincerely, Hurting in this
31   Stupid Town."
32   JOLENE: OK. *(Pause, thinking)* "Dear Hurting in this Stupid
33   Town, This is good news!"
34   LISA: Good news?
35   JOLENE: "Life is about to turn around for you! Because now

1   you can take advantage of the guilt your parents are
2   feeling as they rip their family apart. This is your chance
3   to get everything you want! Your tears, real or fake, will
4   enable your life to become like Christmas every day. Work
5   for a car? Forget it! Your parents will compete to buy you
6   the best car they can. A tattoo? Of course! So believe it or
7   not, you're about to become the most spoiled rotten teen
8   in this stupid town!"
9 LISA: Oh, my gosh! You're insane if you think *The Rising Star*
10   would print something like that!
11 JOLENE: OK, give me another shot at this. Ask me another one.
12 LISA: Just to prove my point that you are a basket case, here it
13   goes. "Dear Jolene, I'm scared. I think I might be
14   pregnant. What should I do? Signed, Unwed and Scared to
15   Death."
16 JOLENE: "Dear Unwed and Scared to Death, Cheer up!"
17 LISA: Cheer up?
18 JOLENE: "Life could be worse. You could be in your forties,
19   married, and have just managed to get your last kid out of
20   the house when you realize the 'oops baby' is on the way."
21 LISA: You are insane!
22 JOLENE: "So my advice to you, Unwed and Scared to Death,
23   deal with it and quit having a pity party. Life goes on so
24   face whatever is ahead and quit whining about it." See,
25   Lisa, instead of giving the readers your typical response,
26   I'll just get down to the nitty gritty truth!
27 LISA: OK, here's one more.
28 JOLENE: Ready!
29 LISA: "Dear Jolene, I need to fire an employee, but she doesn't
30   seem to get it. How do I get it across to her that she is fired?
31   Signed, Desperate Editor."
32 JOLENE: Oh, this is a good one! You may need this answer for a
33   future employee. "Dear Desperate Editor, I suggest you
34   confront your employee, look at him ... or her ... directly in
35   the face and scream at the top of your lungs, 'You

1   are fired!'"
2   LISA: *(Smiles.)* **Excellent advice.**
3   JOLENE: Wait! "Unless you see some potential in that
4   employee, then I'd suggest you give him ... or her ... a
5   second chance."
6   LISA: Oh, we're way past the second chances.
7   JOLENE: Then I say you seek to discover her talent as you work
8   together as a team. They do say that two is better than one,
9   so make her the co-editor and you will watch with
10   amazement as *The Rising Star News* reaches
11   unimaginable heights in readership. Picture this: an
12   entire page, not a little column, but an entire page of
13   personal problems from readers that will spark more
14   interest than ever before. Dear Abby is out and Dear
15   Jolene is in. I wonder if I could get syndicated as well?
16   LISA: Jolene ...
17   JOLENE: Yes?
18   LISA: *You are fired!*
19   JOLENE: Wait! I can be on time! I won't steal any more pets! Just
20   give me another chance, OK? Please! How about this?
21   "Dear Jolene, I've just been fired from a job that I love.
22   What do I do? Signed, Fired for No Reason."
23   LISA: "Dear Fired for No Reason, I have great news for you!"
24   JOLENE: Great news?
25   LISA: Yes! Cheer up! You can sleep till noon if you please! Do
26   nothing all day! And play with any leftover pets you may
27   have! And best of all, your boss can rejoice in being rid of
28   you!
29   JOLENE: Wait! What if you put me in charge of the horoscopes?
30   Listen to this one. Gemini: Today your best friend needs
31   you to listen, so bite your tongue if you feel the urge to
32   offer advice.
33   LISA: No!
34   JOLENE: Sagittarius: Today the new moon drives you to confess
35   your unspoken sins, so be prepared to stay home and

1   seclude yourself.

2   LISA: No!

3   JOLENE: Taurus: Today you must make a difficult decision.

4   Offer a second chance to someone or crush the person

5   who will prove to be irreplaceable.

6   LISA: *You're fired!*

7   JOLENE: OK, that's fine. I guess I'll go write a letter to Dear

8   Abby. We'll see what she has to say about all this! "Dear

9   Abby, you won't believe what happened to me today ... "

10

11

12

13

14

15

16

17

18

19

20

21

22

23

24

25

26

27

28

29

30

31

32

33

34

35

9. New Best Friend Forever

Cast: CLAIRE and PAIGE
Setting: Outside a hospital room

1 CLAIRE: Wait! Let's talk about this before we go in.

2 PAIGE: OK.

3 CLAIRE: What should we say when we go into her room?

4 PAIGE: We'll say she looks wonderful.

5 CLAIRE: *(Practicing)* Haley, you look wonderful!

6 PAIGE: And then I can mention that I recently watched a show

7   on *Medical Miracles* about reconstructive surgery.

8 CLAIRE: Paige, no! Don't mention her nose!

9 PAIGE: But when the swelling goes down, maybe they can fix it.

10 CLAIRE: How?

11 PAIGE: A skin graft I suppose.

12 CLAIRE: I still say it's best not to mention her nose.

13 PAIGE: OK, you're probably right. We'll say she looks

14   wonderful, despite the fact that the tip of her nose is

15   missing.

16 CLAIRE: Do you think there's a bandage on it?

17 PAIGE: I don't know. I hope so. I really wouldn't want to see it

18   uncovered.

19 CLAIRE: Me neither.

20 PAIGE: But maybe they can give her a new nose. Borrow one

21   from someone or something.

22 CLAIRE: Paige, how do you borrow a nose?

23 PAIGE: Think about it, Claire. A donor.

1 CLAIRE: Who leaves a nose? A heart, kidney, lung, sure. But a
2   nose?
3 PAIGE: I don't know. But I'm sure it's done. I once heard of a
4   lady getting an entire face.
5 CLAIRE: I heard about that, too.
6 PAIGE: And this is just one nose! Actually, just the tip of a nose.
7 CLAIRE: Can they transplant just the tip of a nose?
8 PAIGE: Of course they can!
9 CLAIRE: So we'll say she looks wonderful, and then quickly
10   move on to a safe subject like Megan's wedding next
11   weekend.
12 PAIGE: Claire, she may not want to go to Megan's wedding now
13   that she's missing her nose.
14 CLAIRE: Unless they can hurry up and sew on a new one.
15 PAIGE: I think that takes time. They have to find a matching
16   donor and that could take awhile. Maybe months.
17   *(CLAIRE laughs.)* What's so funny?
18 CLAIRE: Wouldn't it be funny if donor noses were on short
19   supply so they had to borrow one from an animal?
20 PAIGE: Like give her a little black puppy nose?
21 CLAIRE: That stayed wet all the time!
22 PAIGE: Or a pig's nose! *(Pushes up her nose and makes oinking*
23   *sounds. They share a laugh.)*
24 CLAIRE: Or an elephant's nose! Trunk and all!
25 PAIGE: Or a horse's nose with these big, huge nostrils!
26 CLAIRE: Or a little twitchy rabbit's nose.
27 PAIGE: That's funny to think about, but I don't think that
28   would ever happen.
29 CLAIRE: But I wonder if Haley talks funny now?
30 PAIGE: What do you mean?
31 CLAIRE: Like this. *(Holds her nostrils together and talks.)* Do you
32   think Haley sounds like this since she's missing part of
33   her nose?
34 PAIGE: Gosh, I hope she doesn't sound like that. Because if she
35   did, I'm afraid I would laugh.

1 CLAIRE: I know. Me too. OK, so we enter the room and say she
2   looks wonderful.
3 PAIGE: And quickly change the subject.
4 CLAIRE: Not mentioning Megan's wedding next week.
5 PAIGE: I know! I'll tell her about my problems with Paul. Let
6   her see that other people are having major life problems
7   besides her. And maybe I'll even exaggerate a bit. So by the
8   time I get through telling her about my problems with
9   Paul, her missing nose will seem minor.
10 CLAIRE: That's a good idea.
11 PAIGE: Let's see ... I'll tell Haley that Paul and I broke up ...
12 CLAIRE: Long time coming.
13 PAIGE: What?
14 CLAIRE: I meant I saw it coming.
15 PAIGE: Why would you say that? You know I love Paul.
16 CLAIRE: So the two of you really did break up?
17 PAIGE: Sort of. I mean, I'm not talking to him right now.
18 CLAIRE: That's not anything new. And Paige, I don't think
19   that's enough to get Haley's mind off her missing nose.
20 PAIGE: Claire, in all actuality, my problem with Paul is more
21   life shattering than Haley's nose.
22 CLAIRE: Do you think Paul would kiss you if you were missing
23   your nose?
24 PAIGE: I'm not talking to Paul right now so I don't know
25   because he wouldn't even have the chance.
26 CLAIRE: OK, what did he do this time?
27 PAIGE: Look, I said I was going to exaggerate a bit so Haley
28   wouldn't think about her nose ... or lack of, that is. So I'll
29   tell Haley that Paul and I broke up because ...
30 CLAIRE: Yes?
31 PAIGE: Because I caught him with another girl.
32 CLAIRE: Really?
33 PAIGE: Yes, and this time ...
34 CLAIRE: This time?
35 PAIGE: I'm trying to make it sound worse than it is, Claire.

1   **CLAIRE: Oh.**

2   **PAIGE: And this time there's no going back. No forgiveness and**
3   **no second chances.**

4   **CLAIRE: Because you reached your limit? He hurt you one too**
5   **many times?**

6   **PAIGE: Yes, but it's much worse than that!**

7   **CLAIRE: Really?**

8   **PAIGE: Guess who Paul cheated on me with?**

9   **CLAIRE: Who?**

10 **PAIGE: Wait. Maybe I should lead up to that part. I'll talk about**
11   **how I've cried for days. Haven't slept. Haven't eaten.**

12 **CLAIRE: You know, you look pretty good for that. Maybe you**
13   **should wipe off some of your makeup.**

14 **PAIGE: Good idea.** *(Attempts to wipe off her makeup.)* **And this is**
15   **what I'll say to Haley. "Haley, you wouldn't believe who I**
16   **caught him with!"**

17 **CLAIRE: Who?**

18 **PAIGE:** *(Points to CLAIRE.)* **Her!**

19 **CLAIRE: Me?**

20 **PAIGE: Yes, her! My best friend in the whole world!**

21 **CLAIRE: Oh, no you don't!**

22 **PAIGE:** *(Still pointing to CLAIRE)* **She was kissing my boyfriend!**
23   **Can you believe that?**

24 **CLAIRE: You leave me out of your exaggerated story!**

25 **PAIGE: And they wouldn't stop! Clinging onto each other,**
26   **kissing as if there were no tomorrow!** *(Looks at CLAIRE.)* **I**
27   **hate you, Claire!**

28 **CLAIRE: Oh, I get it. So if you and I are having a huge fight in**
29   **Haley's room, it'll keep her mind off her nose. Or lack of,**
30   **that is.**

31 **PAIGE: Exactly! And every day or so, you and I can run into**
32   **Haley's room, separately of course, and cry about our**
33   **problems to her. She will be so involved in our soap opera**
34   **lives that she won't have the time to think about her own**
35   **problems.**

1   **CLAIRE: Her missing nose!**

2   **PAIGE: Exactly!**

3   **CLAIRE: You know, that's really not a bad idea. And when she**

4   **gets a new nose and is feeling better, we can tell her the**

5   **truth. We're still best friends.**

6   **PAIGE: Best friends forever. So, do you think we should**

7   **practice? So it appears real?**

8   **CLAIRE: Good idea. OK, so we enter her hospital room.**

9   **PAIGE: Haley, you look wonderful! I didn't even notice your**

10   **missing nose!**

11   **CLAIRE: Don't say that! Of course you noticed it! Let's start**

12   **over.**

13   **PAIGE: OK.** *(Clears throat.)* **Haley, you look wonderful! Did you**

14   **do something different to your hair? Because you look**

15   **radiant! Just radiant!**

16   **CLAIRE: No, Paige, that's going overboard. Just stick to the "you**

17   **look wonderful" part.**

18   **PAIGE: Maybe we shouldn't even mention how she looks. How**

19   **about if I just burst into the room crying?**

20   **CLAIRE: Oh, and that'll make her feel good? She'll think you're**

21   **crying about her nose being gone.**

22   **PAIGE: That's true. OK, so I won't start crying until we start**

23   **arguing over Paul.**

24   **CLAIRE: Good. So why don't you let me be the one to start**

25   **talking.**

26   **PAIGE: OK.**

27   **CLAIRE: Let's practice this again. So we walk into Haley's**

28   **room.** *(Clears throat.)* **Hi, Haley! Paige and I were in the**

29   **neighborhood and thought we'd drop by.**

30   **PAIGE: And Haley, I need to talk to you because my life is falling**

31   **apart!**

32   **CLAIRE: What's wrong?**

33   **PAIGE:** *(To CLAIRE, angrily)* **Don't you play the innocent act**

34   **here, Claire! You know exactly what's going on!**

35   **CLAIRE: No, I don't.**

1   PAIGE: Haley, my life is falling apart and it's all because of
2   someone in this room!
3   CLAIRE: Why don't you just spit it out, Paige, instead of playing
4   these stupid word games?
5   PAIGE: Then why don't you stop sneaking behind my back with
6   my boyfriend, Claire!
7   CLAIRE: It's not my fault.
8   PAIGE: Not your fault?! Not your fault?! I think it is your fault,
9   Claire! Because you knew Paul is weak when it comes to
10   other women and you just had to throw yourself at him,
11   didn't you?
12   CLAIRE: Oh, believe me, I didn't have to throw myself at him!
13   The truth is, Paul threw himself at me!
14   PAIGE: You liar!
15   CLAIRE: And by the way, we're in love!
16   PAIGE: You can't love him!
17   CLAIRE: Sorry, but it's too late!
18   PAIGE: But I love him!
19   CLAIRE: Well, then I guess we both love him! But the question
20   is, who does Paul love? Answer? Me!
21   PAIGE: Haley, do you see what Claire is doing to me? Do you?
22   *(Looks at CLAIRE.)* How could you?
23   CLAIRE: I'm sorry, but Paul and I couldn't fight it any longer.
24   We had a connection that couldn't be controlled.
25   PAIGE: And what about me?
26   CLAIRE: We can still be friends.
27   PAIGE: Oh, no we can't!
28   CLAIRE: Oh well. You win some, you lose some.
29   PAIGE: So, you're willing to give up our friendship so you can
30   chase my boyfriend?
31   CLAIRE: Paige, he chased me and I, well, I couldn't resist.
32   PAIGE: You ... you ... you ... ! We are finished! Finished! Haley,
33   you'll be my new best friend forever, won't you?
34   CLAIRE: No! Haley's going to be my new best friend forever!
35   Right, Haley?

1   PAIGE: Hey, this is good. With you and I fighting for her friendship,
2   she won't even think twice about her missing nose.
3   CLAIRE: This is a good idea. And seriously, you really do need
4   to end things with Paul.
5   PAIGE: Why?
6   CLAIRE: Because he's not your type.
7   PAIGE: Yes he is!
8   CLAIRE: No he's not.
9   PAIGE: What? Is he your type?
10 CLAIRE: He's more my type than yours. Paige, you need a
11   serious, even-tempered, laid-back type of guy. And I like
12   them a little rowdy and wild.
13 PAIGE: Like Paul?
14 CLAIRE: Yeah, like Paul.
15 PAIGE: Oh really? So you're telling me that you like my rowdy
16   and wild boyfriend?
17 CLAIRE: I'm saying that he's more my type than your type. You
18   want to hold him down and I'd let him be free.
19 PAIGE: With you?
20 CLAIRE: I didn't say that.
21 PAIGE: So, tell me, Claire. Have you and my boyfriend ever
22   done anything?
23 CLAIRE: Like what?
24 PAIGE: Like anything!
25 CLAIRE: You mean outside of running into each other?
26 PAIGE: I mean, have you ever been alone with him on purpose?
27 CLAIRE: Been alone with Paul on purpose?
28 PAIGE: Just answer the question!
29 CLAIRE: Well ... once.
30 PAIGE: Once?
31 CLAIRE: Once at a movie. OK, twice. There was the coffee shop.
32   And the time at my house. But that was just to talk.
33 PAIGE: I can't believe this! You really did cheat with Paul?
34 CLAIRE: I didn't cheat! I was available. He's the one who
35   cheated!

1   **PAIGE: Why, you ... you ... you ... You know what? I am going into**

2   **Haley's room and tell her what you did! Then I'm going to**

3   **see if she will be my new best friend forever! Because we**

4   **are finished, Claire! In real life, you and I are finished!**

5   **CLAIRE: It wasn't me, Paige! It was him!**

6   **PAIGE: But you ... you ... you ... Oh!**

7   **CLAIRE: No, if we're finished, then I'm asking Haley to be my**

8   **new best friend!**

9   **PAIGE: No, I am!**

10   **CLAIRE: No, I am...**

11   **PAIGE:** *(As they both rush into the room)* **Haley, you won't**

12   **believe what Claire did!**

13   **CLAIRE: Haley, don't listen to her! It wasn't my fault!**

14

15

16

17

18

19

20

21

22

23

24

25

26

27

28

29

30

31

32

33

34

35

10. The Singing Telegram

Cast: KYLIE and JENNA
Setting: The front door of Jenna's home
Props: paper, pen

1   **KYLIE: Hello, are you Jenna Reeves?**

2   **JENNA: Yes, I am. Why?**

3   **KYLIE: Delivery!**

4   **JENNA: You have a delivery for me?**

5   **KYLIE: Yes.**

6   **JENNA: Flowers?**

7   **KYLIE: No.**

8   **JENNA: Not court papers, I hope.**

9   **KYLIE: No.**

10 **JENNA: Well, then what's my delivery?**

11 **KYLIE:** *(Clears her throat, glances at a piece of paper, and then*

12   *begins singing very badly.)* **I'm sorry to do it this way, sorry**

13   **to do it this way, but you wouldn't talk to me, refused to**

14   **answer my calls, deleted my e-mails, I'm sure —**

15 **JENNA: Wait! What is this? A singing telegram?**

16 **KYLIE:** *(Nods, clears throat and glances back to notes.)* **So this is**

17   **my last attempt to tell you** *(Operatic)* **I'm sorry ... so very**

18   **sorry ... And please ... please forgive me!**

19 **JENNA: That was bad.**

20 **KYLIE: I'm sorry. Jobs have been scarce and well, they hired**

21   **me.**

22 **JENNA: I just want to know one thing.**

23 **KYLIE: Yes?**

1 JENNA: Who is that from?

2 KYLIE: You don't know?

3 JENNA: How would I know?

4 KYLIE: *(Looks at notes.)* Oh, no!

5 JENNA: What?

6 KYLIE: I forgot to write down the customer's name. Paid up
7   front, handed me this letter, well, this song, and I forgot to
8   get the name.

9 JENNA: Are you telling me you don't know who it's from?

10 KYLIE: I'm sorry, but somehow I forgot that one small detail.

11 JENNA: What kind of singing telegram person are you?

12 KYLIE: Wait. Let me double check. *(Looks over notes again.)* No,
13   it's not here.

14 JENNA: Which means that whoever paid for this singing
15   telegram should get a refund!

16 KYLIE: I would, but —

17 JENNA: But you don't know who it's from!

18 KYLIE: I'm sorry. I don't know how this happened.

19 JENNA: And you really don't remember who hired you?

20 KYLIE: I don't. I get so many.

21 JENNA: You get a lot of singing telegrams?

22 KYLIE: You can't even imagine. Birthdays, anniversaries,
23   wedding proposals ... and obviously apologies.

24 JENNA: So how am I supposed to decide if that apology is
25   accepted if I don't know who it's from?

26 KYLIE: My mistake.

27 JENNA: Can you try to narrow it down for me? Male? Female?

28 KYLIE: As I said, I get a lot of these.

29 JENNA: Well, think! Think real hard!

30 KYLIE: *(Closes eyes.)* OK. I'm thinking.

31 JENNA: Man or woman?

32 KYLIE: I think it was a man.

33 JENNA: Dark hair, brown, blonde, red?

34 KYLIE: Dark.

35 JENNA: Facial hair? Moustache? Beard?

1   **KYLIE: No.**

2   **JENNA: Piercings?**

3   **KYLIE: No.**

4   **JENNA: Tattoos?**

5   **KYLIE: No.**

6   **JENNA: Short? Tall?**

7   **KYLIE: Average.**

8   **JENNA: Thin? Heavy?**

9   **KYLIE: Average.**

10 **JENNA: Age?**

11 **KYLIE: I'm not a good judge of people's ages. Once I thought**

12   **this lady was in her twenties and she was fourteen-years-**

13   **old.**

14 **JENNA: Well, is there anything else that stands out about this**

15   **man who hired you?**

16 **KYLIE: Actually ...**

17 **JENNA: Yes?**

18 **KYLIE: It could have been a woman.**

19 **JENNA: You don't remember, do you?**

20 **KYLIE: No. I told you I didn't. But maybe if you listen to the**

21   **song once again it might give you a clue as to who it's**

22   **from. *(Clears throat. Sings.)* I'm sorry to do it this way,**

23   **sorry to do it this way, but you wouldn't talk to me, refused**

24   **to answer my calls, deleted my e-mails, I'm sure. So this is**

25   **my last attempt to tell you *(Operatic)* I'm sorry, so very**

26   **sorry. And please, please forgive me!**

27 **JENNA: That could be from anyone!**

28 **KYLIE: Anyone? How many people are you mad at?**

29 **JENNA: How many? Well, let's see. There's Judy from work,**

30   **Christy from my poetry club, Matt my ex-boyfriend, that**

31   **lady at the checkout line who rammed her cart into the**

32   **back of my heel ... oh, and my mother!**

33 **KYLIE: Your mother?**

34 **JENNA: Yes! But I wonder ... would my mother send me a**

35   **singing telegram?**

1 KYLIE: I've had mothers as customers. Seems like just
2   yesterday ...
3 JENNA: Is that when you got hired to do my telegram?
4 KYLIE: Yes, it was yesterday. I do remember that.
5 JENNA: And you remember talking to an older woman with
6   short gray hair ... glasses ... about this tall, and ...
7 KYLIE: No. I'm sorry, but I don't remember. I get so many.
8 JENNA: Exactly how many did you get yesterday?
9 KYLIE: *(Counting on fingers)* One ... two ... three. Three.
10 JENNA: You only got three orders for singing telegrams and you
11   can't remember who hired you?
12 KYLIE: I can't. It was a crazy day. Miranda was out of the office
13   so I was answering the phone and setting up
14   appointments and rushing out the door for one
15   emergency singing telegram.
16 JENNA: An emergency singing telegram?
17 KYLIE: Yes. Some guy forgot his wife's birthday and he paid
18   double for a rush. *(Clears throat.)* Happy birthday to you,
19   happy birthday to you, happy birthday dear Josephine,
20   happy birthday to you!
21 JENNA: Back to my singing telegram.
22 KYLIE: Would you like to hear it again?
23 JENNA: No! But I would like to know who it's from! So think,
24   think really hard.
25 KYLIE: OK.
26 JENNA: Was my telegram ordered before or after your
27   emergency telegram?
28 KYLIE: *(Confident)* Before. I think.
29 JENNA: And you don't know if it was my mother?
30 KYLIE: I never met your mother so I wouldn't know that.
31   Unless of course she was the one who hired me. But I don't
32   remember.
33 JENNA: Oh, this is frustrating! The one time in my life I get a
34   singing telegram and the horrible singer here can't even
35   tell me who it's from!

1   **KYLIE: I have an idea!**

2   **JENNA: What?**

3   **KYLIE: This time when I sing it to you, pay very close attention**

4   **to the words and think about who would have said those**

5   **words to you.**

6   **JENNA: Well, I guess we can give it one more shot.**

7   **KYLIE:** *(Clears throat.)* **I'm sorry to do it this way, sorry to do it**

8   **this way, but you wouldn't talk to me, refused to answer**

9   **my calls, deleted my e-mails, I'm sure. So this is my last**

10   **attempt to tell you** *(Operatic)* **I'm sorry, so very sorry. And**

11   **please, please forgive me!** *(Regular voice)* **Now you should**

12   **know who it's from!**

13   **JENNA: Well, I don't!**

14   **KYLIE: Well, whose phone calls are you ignoring?**

15   **JENNA: There's Judy from work, Christy from my poetry club,**

16   **Matt my ex-boyfriend, that lady at the checkout line who**

17   **rammed her cart into the back of my heel, but I don't**

18   **think she has my phone number.**

19   **KYLIE: And your mother.**

20   **JENNA: And my mother!**

21   **KYLIE: So that's four people that the telegram could have come**

22   **from. So, who do you think it's from?**

23   **JENNA: I don't know, Miss Singing Telegram Person! Why don't**

24   **you tell me who it's from since you're the one who got**

25   **hired to sing to me! And badly might I add.**

26   **KYLIE: I wish I could, but somehow I failed to write down the**

27   **giver's name.**

28   **JENNA: Which means someone deserves a refund.**

29   **KYLIE: True, but if I don't know who it's from that would be**

30   **very hard to do, don't you think?**

31   **JENNA: Then you should give the refund to me. Seems only fair.**

32   **KYLIE: But —**

33   **JENNA: But instead of paying me, you can pay me with singing**

34   **telegrams. Four to be exact.**

35   **KYLIE: You want me to give you four singing telegrams for the**

1   price of one?

2   JENNA: Yes I do.

3   KYLIE: But that doesn't seem fair.

4   JENNA: It seems fair to me. For my pain and suffering of not

5   knowing who my apology was from. And besides all that,

6   if you don't I will call your office and let your boss know

7   what you did. Then I will call the Better Business Bureau.

8   And then —

9   KYLIE: All right, all right, all right! I'll give you four singing

10   telegrams if that'll make you happy.

11   JENNA: You have something to write with?

12   KYLIE: *(Pulls out pad of paper and pen from pocket.)* **Ready.**

13   JENNA: Write down what I tell you and then deliver these in a

14   singing telegram. Sing it badly if you want ... well, not that

15   you have a choice in that matter, but I don't care. Good or

16   bad, I just want my messages delivered.

17   KYLIE: Ready.

18   JENNA: This is for Judy at work. Judy, oh dear, Judy ...

19   KYLIE: *(Sings and writes)* Judy, oh dear, Judy ...

20   JENNA: I wish your cubicle would catch on fire!

21   KYLIE: I wish your cubicle would catch on fire!

22   JENNA: And would I rush in to save you?

23   KYLIE: And would I rush in to save you?

24   JENNA: Or dial nine-one-one?

25   KYLIE: Or dial nine-one-one?

26   JENNA: No!

27   KYLIE: *(Operatic)* **No!**

28   JENNA: I would smile.

29   KYLIE: *(Operatic)* I would smile!

30   JENNA: Because you are a two-faced lying snake!

31   KYLIE: *(Operatic)* Because you are a two-faced lying snake!

32   JENNA: Perfect. OK, ready for the next one?

33   KYLIE: Ready.

34   JENNA: This is for Christy from my poetry club. Christy,

35   dear Christy ...

1   **KYLIE:** *(Sings and writes.)* **Christy, dear Christy ...**

2   **JENNA: Who loves to critique my poetry.**

3   **KYLIE: Who loves to critique my poetry.**

4   **JENNA: Who describes my poems as big words splattered on**
5   **paper ...**

6   **KYLIE: ... big words splattered on paper ...**

7   **JENNA: Resembling garbage.**

8   **KYLIE:** *(Operatic)* **Resembling garbage!**

9   **JENNA: And here's my line to you...**

10   **KYLIE:** *(Operatic)* **... my line to you ...**

11   **JENNA: Your poetry ...**

12   **KYLIE: Your poetry ...**

13   **JENNA: Is dull, redundant, dry, and without rhyme!**

14   **KYLIE:** *(Operatic)* **... dull ... redundant ... dry ... and without**
15   **rhyme!**

16   **JENNA: Good. And now to my ex-boyfriend's telegram. Ready?**

17   **KYLIE: Ready.**

18   **JENNA: Matt, dear Matt ...**

19   **KYLIE:** *(Sings and writes.)* **Matt, dear Matt ...**

20   **JENNA: The exes of all exes.**

21   **KYLIE: The exes of all exes.**

22   **JENNA: The scummiest of the scum ...**

23   **KYLIE: The scummiest of the scum ...**

24   **JENNA: Who is dating my niece, Hannah ...**

25   **KYLIE: Who is dating my niece Hannah ...**

26   **JENNA: Matt, dear Matt ... I have one word for you ...**

27   **KYLIE: ... have one word for you ...**

28   **JENNA: I hate you!**

29   **KYLIE: Wait.**

30   **JENNA: What?**

31   **KYLIE:** *I hate you* **is three words.**

32   **JENNA: Then say three words!**

33   **KYLIE:** *(Writes down changes, then sings.)* **I have three words for**
34   **you ...** *(Operatic)* ***I hate you!***

35   **JENNA: Good. Now for my mother. Mother, dear Mother ...**

1   **KYLIE:** *(Sings and writes.)* **Mother, dear Mother ...**
2   **JENNA: You have ruined my life ...**
3   **KYLIE: ... ruined my life ...**
4   **JENNA: The curfews, strict rules ...**
5   **KYLIE: curfews, strict rules ...**
6   **JENNA: Master of perfection ...**
7   **KYLIE: Master of perfection ...**
8   **JENNA: Killer of dreams ...**
9   **KYLIE:** *(Operatic)* **Killer of dreams ...** *(Goes on without help)*
10   **Killer of dreams, Mother, oh Mother ... who caused me to**
11   **feel ugly, withdrawn, and unloved ... who left me with a**
12   **mountain of anger ... whom no one could love ... yes, no**
13   **one could love, no one could love at all!**
14   **JENNA: Excuse me?**
15   **KYLIE:** *(Still singing)* **I have a word for you ... No. I have three**
16   **words for you! I hate you! Oh, Mother ... I hate you! I hate**
17   **you ... I hate you ... I hate you!** *(Pauses.)* **How was that?**
18   **JENNA: That's not what I said! I can't tell my mother I hate her!**
19   **Don't say that. I just want to say that I'm mad at her. I'm**
20   **mad at her for being so strict and unwavering and ... and**
21   **expecting the best from me!**
22   **KYLIE:** *(Writing and singing)* **Killer of dreams ...**
23   **JENNA: No, leave that part out.**
24   **KYLIE:** *(Looks up.)* **It's what you said.**
25   **JENNA: Just say ...**
26   **KYLIE: Yes?**
27   **JENNA: Say that I'm sorry.**
28   **KYLIE: Sorry? You want to tell your mother that you're sorry?**
29   **JENNA: Yes. I was a rebellious teen who was completely**
30   **unmanageable.**
31   **KYLIE:** *(Writing and singing)* **Sorry, so very, very sorry ...**
32   **JENNA: That should do it.**
33   **KYLIE: OK, I think I've got it all here.** *(Looking at her pages of*
34   *scribbled notes)* **Judy from work, Christy from the poetry**
35   **club, Matt your ex-boyfriend, and Mother ... oh, dear**

1   Mother. Oh, wait, look! What's this?

2 JENNA: What?

3 KYLIE: Who's Ralph?

4 JENNA: Ralph?

5 KYLIE: Ralph Sparkman.

6 JENNA: Ralph Sparkman? That's my ex-ex-boyfriend. How did

7   you know his name?

8 KYLIE: Ralph Sparkman! I did write it down! The singing

9   telegram was from him!

10 JENNA: But I'm not speaking to Ralph, that scumbag!

11 KYLIE: Not answering his phone calls? Deleting his e-mails?

12 JENNA: Yes!

13 KYLIE: The telegram was from him. *(Sings.)* I'm sorry to do it

14   this way, sorry to do it this way, but you wouldn't talk to

15   me, refused to answer my calls, deleted my e-mails, I'm

16   sure. So this is my last attempt to tell you *(Operatic)* I'm

17   sorry, so very sorry. And please, please forgive me! From

18   Ralph Sparkman. Your ex-ex-boyfriend.

19 JENNA: He still loves me?

20 KYLIE: Apparently so.

21 JENNA: Oh, Ralph ...

22 KYLIE: And these four credits you just asked for ... Judy, Christy,

23   Matt, and dear, oh dear Mother ... well, you can forget it!

24   No refunds for you, missy!

25 JENNA: He still loves me?

26 KYLIE: I guess so.

27 JENNA: Wait! Before you leave could you do me a favor?

28 KYLIE: What's that?

29 JENNA: Could you sing the telegram to me once more? Now that

30   I know who it's from?

31 KYLIE: Well, I suppose, since I did cause you so much

32   confusion.

33 JENNA: Thank you.

34 KYLIE: *(Clears throat.)* I'm sorry to do it this way, sorry to do it

35   this way, but you wouldn't talk to me, refused to answer

1   **my calls, deleted my e-mails, I'm sure. So this is my last**

2   **attempt to tell you** *(Operatic)* **I'm sorry, so very sorry. And**

3   **please, please forgive me!** *(Goes on as she is getting into it)*

4   **Please, please, please, please forgive me! I'm begging.**

5   *(Gets down on one knee.)* **Down on my knee. Please, please,**

6   **please. Oh, please forgive me!** *(JENNA gives her a strange*

7   *look, then exits.)*

8

9

10

11

12

13

14

15

16

17

18

19

20

21

22

23

24

25

26

27

28

29

30

31

32

33

34

35

11. Modern Day Odd Couple

Cast: JULIA and ALLIE
Setting: A small apartment in New York City
Props: phone, pair of black boots

1   JULIA: Allie, have you seen my black Gucci boots?

2   ALLIE: Why are you asking me?

3   JULIA: Have you seen them? I have an audition this afternoon

4   and I need to find them.

5   ALLIE: Not my problem.

6   JULIA: Allie, why do you have such an attitude?

7   ALLIE: Because, Julia, you're a complete slob and I'm sick of it.

8   JULIA: Do not start on me. I don't have time for this.

9   ALLIE: Poor Mom. She always tried so hard with you.

10 JULIA: Finding my black Gucci boots has nothing to do with

11   Mom!

12 ALLIE: She hoped you'd outgrow your sloppiness. Did

13   everything she could short of beating you, but nothing

14   worked. And it looks like nothing ever will. And why, why

15   did I agree to share an apartment with my sister in New

16   York?

17 JULIA: To split the rent. And if you'll remember, Allie, it was

18   your idea.

19 ALLIE: And again I ask why?

20 JULIA: Tell me. Do you have any idea where my boots are?

21 ALLIE: I don't. But I do know this: They are not on my side of

22   the apartment. Because my side of the apartment is clean.

1 But you know that. Just look around. Everything is orderly
2 over here. Magazines stacked up, DVDs arranged properly,
3 keys on the hook where they belong, coat on the rack
4 where it belongs, but on your side ... clothes strewn
5 everywhere, papers, receipts, mail all tossed aside to land
6 wherever they may. One shoe here, one shoe there ... You
7 know your Gucci boots might be in two different places.
8 I'd say that's a high possibility given your inability to put
9 anything where it belongs.
10 JULIA: Can you please stop this and help me look for my boots?
11 ALLIE: Honestly, Julia, I'm afraid.
12 JULIA: Afraid to help me find my boots?
13 ALLIE: Of what I might find over there.
14 JULIA: Please, Allie!
15 ALLIE: The last time I helped you look for a lost item I found a
16 roach hotel full of dead roaches next to the green, moldy,
17 half-eaten burger.
18 JULIA: I meant to throw those things away. But the roach motel
19 might have still had some purpose.
20 ALLIE: No, I think it was pretty much booked up.
21 JULIA: I threw it out!
22 ALLIE: After I screamed when a roach fell out.
23 JULIA: Yeah, well it was dead!
24 ALLIE: I don't care for roaches. Dead or alive. Julia, your boots
25 could be anywhere in here. Under the piles of laundry,
26 behind that bag of potting soil, hiding next to your dead
27 plants, stuffed in a cabinet —
28 JULIA: I know! Let's make a game out of it. Whoever finds my
29 boots first gets a dinner of her choice!
30 ALLIE: Right. Which means if you find your own boots first, I
31 have to buy you dinner? I don't think so.
32 JULIA: Allie, please!
33 ALLIE: Julia, you're on your own. Good luck.
34 JULIA: What about this? If you find my boots, or even one boot,
35 I'll do your laundry on Saturday.

1 ALLIE: No thank you. Like I told you, I'm afraid to look for
2   them because of what I might find. You know, we're like
3   the modern day odd couple. The slob and the
4   perfectionist. I'm just glad I'm me and not you.
5 JULIA: You're mean!
6 ALLIE: No, I'm organized.
7 JULIA: OK, Allie, big sister of mine, what will it take?
8 ALLIE: A bulldozer.
9 JULIA: No, for you to help me find my Gucci boots!
10 ALLIE: I know. You start searching for your boots and if you
11   find them within ten minutes, I'll give you a reward.
12 JULIA: What kind of reward?
13 ALLIE: This kind. *(Pats her back.)* Good job, Julia! You've
14   managed to find your boots in the piles of God-knows-
15   what in your half of the apartment.
16 JULIA: Forget it!
17 ALLIE: Thank you and good luck.
18 JULIA: And the next time you need me to tell Rudolph, the big-
19   nosed neighbor who loves the very sight of you, that
20   you're not home, I will just invite him inside for a little
21   visit. And you know his visits can last for hours! And you
22   know, I bet Rudolph would even volunteer to help me
23   clean up my side of the apartment just to be close to you.
24   Of course it might take weeks of us working on it, but it
25   might be fun. And it'd sure be nice to have the help.
26 ALLIE: Julia, you wouldn't!
27 JULIE: This audition is important to me, Allie! I really want this
28   part! It's a play about the life of Marilyn Monroe. And I
29   think I'm perfect for the part. "Diamonds are a girl's best
30   friend." I love that quote, don't you? Or how about this
31   one? "Give a girl the right shoes and she can conquer the
32   world."
33 ALLIE: Really? You? Marilyn Monroe?
34 JULIA: Yes! Or how about this quote of hers? It's in the play. Tell
35   me what you think, OK? *(Pauses as she prepares herself.*

1   *Dramatic)* "I'm selfish, impatient, and a little insecure. I

2   make mistakes, I am out of control, and sometimes hard

3   to handle. But if you can't handle me at my worst, then

4   you sure don't deserve me at my best."

5 ALLIE: Uh ...

6 JULIA: Want to hear another one?

7 ALLIE: No, I don't think —

8 JULIA: Last one. *(Dramatic)* "Beneath the makeup and behind

9   the smile I am just a girl who wishes for the world." Good,

10   huh? I'm sure I'll get the part.

11 ALLIE: And I wish you the best, little sister.

12 JULIA: And anyway, I need my black Gucci boots to make a good

13   impression. But you said you wouldn't help me, so ...

14 ALLIE: That's right.

15 JULIA: And I say Rudolph, the big-nosed neighbor will be

16   invited over tonight.

17 ALLIE: Julia!

18 JULIA: In fact, I bet if I called him right now he'd rush right

19   over here to save the day.

20 ALLIE: And you wouldn't be embarrassed?

21 JULIA: About?

22 ALLIE: Your bra hanging across the computer screen, the

23   candy in the empty ice tray, the fourteen purses scattered

24   across the floor, along with your wardrobe, not to

25   mention the smelly glass of milk turned cottage cheese on

26   your dresser. You wouldn't be the least bit embarrassed?

27 JULIA: No. I'll just tell Rudolph that I've just been so busy with

28   the last play I was in that I couldn't find a spare moment

29   to clean. And I'll tell Rudolph he's such a sweetheart for

30   rushing over to help me and how I'm most certain that my

31   sister Allie appreciates it as well ... seeing that I'm her

32   favorite sister.

33 ALLIE: You're my only sister, Julia!

34 JULIA: Whatever.

35 ALLIE: And you actually think Rudolph would just run over

1   and volunteer to shovel through your filth?
2   JULIA: Of course he would. We both know he's madly in love
3   with you. And like I said, I'll start inviting him over more
4   often. Not like it's a payback or anything for not helping
5   me out. And you know, with all the time Rudolph starts
6   spending over here at our apartment, why, I bet the two of
7   you will be dating in no time. Rudolph will grow on you
8   like mold on a piece of bread.
9   ALLIE: I refuse to be bribed like this!
10 JULIA: Don't worry about it, Allie. It's OK. *(Picks up the phone.)*
11 ALLIE: What are you doing?
12 JULIA: Calling Rudolph. *(Dials and listens.)* Hello, Rudolph, this
13   is Julia from the third floor.
14 ALLIE: No, Julia!
15 JULIA: Hold on. *(Covers phone with hand.)* You'll help me?
16 ALLIE: Yes, but I'm going to pay you back for this, little sister!
17 JULIA: *(Into the phone)* Rudolph, I'll have to call you back.
18   *(Hangs up. Smiles.)* Where do you want to start?
19 ALLIE: I'll start over here and you ... well, just start wherever
20   you want. And hopefully we'll meet in the middle with
21   two Gucci boots.
22 JULIA: Perfect.
23 ALLIE: Just what I wanted to do this afternoon. *(Takes a few steps*
24   *forward. Looking down, she kicks things around on the floor.)*
25 JULIA: What are you doing?
26 ALLIE: Trying not to touch anything. *(Continues to kick things*
27   *out of the way.)* You missing a dead goldfish?
28 JULIA: *(Rushes over.)* Pete? Oh, Pete! I was wondering what
29   happened to you!
30 ALLIE: Apparently he jumped out of the fish tank.
31 JULIA: Pete, why did you do that?
32 ALLIE: Maybe he wanted to help you look for your boots.
33 JULIA: That's not funny! *(Kneels down.)* Ahhhh, Pete. *(Looks up*
34   *at ALLIE.)* We need to have a memorial service this
35   evening.

1   ALLIE: Again? Last month it was Betsy.

2   JULIA: Don't remind me. I went to the tank to feed them and

3   there was Betsy, floating on top of the aquarium. Oh ...

4   and tonight we will mourn poor little Pete. Will you sing a

5   song like you did last time?

6   ALLIE: If we can make it quick. I need to pay some bills and

7   start my taxes. I'll sing "Candle in the Wind" and then we

8   can send poor Pete off to sea.

9   JULIA: Ah ... Pete. *(Stands.)* OK, OK, back to the project at hand.

10   *(Moves to the other side. After a moment)* My bracelet!

11   There you are!

12   ALLIE: *(Still kicking things around with her feet)* Missing a

13   Christmas gift with no gift tag?

14   JULIA: You found it?

15   ALLIE: On the floor. Somehow it didn't make it under the tree

16   this year, did it?

17   JULIA: It was yours.

18   ALLIE: A few months late, wouldn't you say?

19   JULIA: Sorry.

20   ALLIE: What is it?

21   JULIA: Chocolate covered cherries.

22   ALLIE: Probably a little hard now, don't you think?

23   JULIA: Sorry.

24   ALLIE: *(Shakes head, kicking things around on the floor.)* You

25   need to do laundry.

26   JULIA: I know. Oh! There's my favorite lipstick!

27   ALLIE: See any black Gucci boots?

28   JULIA: Not yet.

29   ALLIE: Me neither. There's a brown flip-flop.

30   JULIA: Just one?

31   ALLIE: What do you think?

32   JULIA: Oh well.

33   ALLIE: And a Save the Whales poster.

34   JULIA: Where did that come from?

35   ALLIE: Why are you asking me? This is your side of the

1   apartment. *(Still kicking)* **Pizza** box. Stuffed monkey.

2   Umbrella. Chicken wing. Book on how to organize your

3   life. You should read it, you know?

4 JULIA: Yeah. Hey! My CD! I was looking for this!

5 ALLIE: A white tennis shoe with dried blood on it.

6 JULIA: Oh, that was the day I cut myself shaving my legs.

7 ALLIE: With your tennis shoes on?

8 JULIA: I was in a hurry.

9 ALLIE: So when was the last time you wore your Gucci boots?

10 JULIA: Hmmmm ... let me think ...

11 ALLIE: Wasn't it Saturday when you went on your date with

12   Paul?

13 JULIA: Seems like it.

14 ALLIE: Then you came home and ... ?

15 JULIA: Let me think. I would've come home and plopped on the

16   sofa to tell you about my date. And while I was sitting

17   there I would have taken off my boots. *(They look toward*

18   *the sofa.)*

19 ALLIE: They're not there.

20 JULIA: But wait! You weren't here so I ... let's see ...

21 ALLIE: Think hard.

22 JULIA: I decided to check the mail.

23 ALLIE: And then?

24 JULIA: And then I saw Christy outside and she invited me in for

25   a soda. That's it! I took my boots off at Christy's!

26 ALLIE: So your boots are at Christy's?

27 JULIA: No. I put them back on before coming home.

28 ALLIE: Then you came inside and ... ?

29 JULIA: I walked in the door and I ... let's see ... what did I do? I

30   know! I was so tired and wanted to go to bed. So, I threw

31   off my coat ...

32 ALLIE: Which probably ended up on the floor, correct?

33 JULIA: I found it on top of my monitor the next morning.

34 ALLIE: So you probably took off your boots and threw them as

35   well.

1   JULIA: Probably. *(They look around the room.)*

2   ALLIE: Think. Where did you throw your boots?

3   JULIA: I don't remember.

4   ALLIE: Next to your bed?

5   JULIA: Already looked there.

6   ALLIE: In your closet?

7   JULIA: Already looked.

8   ALLIE: On top of the mounds of dirty laundry?

9   JULIA: I checked there first.

10 ALLIE: Then your boots must have sprouted legs and walked

11   away.

12 JULIA: Or someone stole them!

13 ALLIE: Don't look at me!

14 JULIA: You didn't borrow them?

15 ALLIE: No. I have my own boots.

16 JULIA: Then where could they be?

17 ALLIE: I don't know, Julia! So you walked in the apartment and

18   tossed your coat and ... ?

19 JULIA: I remember taking off my boots because my feet were

20   hurting.

21 ALLIE: And then you ... ?

22 JULIA: Oh yeah! I went to the kitchen for a snack!

23 ALLIE: Still carrying your boots?

24 JULIA: Maybe.

25 ALLIE: What did you have for a snack?

26 JULIA: I pulled some baby carrots out of the bottom veggie tray.

27 ALLIE: Go look.

28 JULIA: *(Exits then returns with a pair of boots.)* Found them!

29 ALLIE: *(Shakes head.)* I'm calling Mom.

30 JULIA: You're going to tattle on me?

31 ALLIE: I'm going to ask her to let you move back home.

32 JULIA: Because I misplaced my Gucci boots?

33 ALLIE: Because you don't know your boots don't belong in the

34   refrigerator!

35 JULIA: Well, they're a little cold, but at least I found them!

1   **ALLIE:** *(As she exits)* **I'm calling Mom.**

2   **JULIA: If you're calling Mom, then I'm calling Rudolph! What**

3   **do you think about that? Huh? Huh? Oh, whatever.** *(Puts*

4   *on the boots, then quotes Marilyn Monroe.)* **"Give a girl the**

5   **right shoes and she can conquer the world."**

6

7

8

9

10

11

12

13

14

15

16

17

18

19

20

21

22

23

24

25

26

27

28

29

30

31

32

33

34

35

12. Fake-A-Roo

Cast: TAYLOR and MAGGIE
Setting: An alley
Props: letter

1 TAYLOR: What is this? You're alive?

2 MAGGIE: Yes, I am! I did the ole fake-a-roo!

3 TAYLOR: You faked your own death?

4 MAGGIE: I did! Look! I'm alive!

5 TAYLOR: I thought it was a terrible joke when I got a text from
6   *your* phone. "Meet me in the alley behind Fredrick's. I'm
7   not dead. Don't tell anyone."

8 MAGGIE: Taylor, it wasn't a joke. I sent you that text. See! I'm
9   alive!

10 TAYLOR: So, where have you been?

11 MAGGIE: I checked into a hotel room.

12 TAYLOR: Well, no wonder they couldn't find your body.

13 MAGGIE: Isn't it amazing? I didn't drown after all!

14 TAYLOR: This sounds like a soap opera.

15 MAGGIE: Actually, that's where I got the idea. On *City of*
16   *Shame,* my favorite soap opera of all time, Nicole faked
17   her own death to make John realize that it was her he
18   actually loved and not that ruthless and mean-spirited
19   Holly. See, the minute John thought Nicole was dead, he
20   fell apart and realized he'd let the one thing go that he
21   truly loved. Sure, Holly tried to console him, but he was
22   inconsolable. And when Nicole miraculously showed up
23   at her own funeral a couple days later, you could've heard
24   a pin drop. Was she a ghost or was Nicole truly standing in
25   front of her own coffin? When John realized it was her, he

1   ran into her arms, kissed her, picked her up, and carried
2   her out of the chapel. It was a happily-ever-after ending!
3   Well, it was for a couple of days until Holly locked Nicole
4   in a basement then rushed to John to tell him they were
5   going to be having a baby, even though she wasn't even
6   pregnant and knew she was going to have to fake this
7   whole pregnancy thing. And in the meantime, Holly was
8   still being held prisoner, and then —
9 TAYLOR: Wait a minute! Are you telling me that you plan to
10   show up at your own funeral?
11 MAGGIE: I am! Isn't it exciting? And wild?
12 TAYLOR: What? You're just going to walk in and say, "Surprise!
13   I'm not dead!"
14 MAGGIE: Well, no, not like that. I'm going to wear a long black
15   dress and a big black hat so that no one recognizes me.
16   Then I'll sit at the very back so I can watch how everyone
17   reacts to the thought of me being dead. Then at the
18   appropriate time, as everyone is crying and boo-hooing, I
19   will stand up, walk to the front of the chapel, pull off my
20   hat, and look out to all my grieving friends and say, "I'm
21   here, everyone! I'm here! So dry your tears and let's
22   celebrate."
23 TAYLOR: What about your parents?
24 MAGGIE: They're overseas. By the time they return, I'll be back
25   from the dead.
26 TAYLOR: I can't believe you're doing this!
27 MAGGIE: Isn't it exciting? I mean, how many people get to
28   attend their own funeral? Except for the people in the
29   soap operas. But I'm going to do it! I'm going to sit in the
30   back of that chapel and listen to all the wailing. Of course
31   my eyes will mostly be focused on David. I can't wait to see
32   him cry over me. I can hear him now. *(Wails.)* "Oh, Maggie,
33   Maggie, how could I have ever let you go? You were the
34   love of my life and I let you slip away! If only I had one last
35   chance with you! But now ... now ... " *(Wails.)* And of course

1   it'll be nice to see everyone else fall apart over me, too.

2   Like Jessica and Tate and Christina.

3 TAYLOR: Christina said she couldn't make it. She has a biology

4   final tomorrow and can't miss the exam.

5 MAGGIE: What? Not even for her best friend's funeral?

6 TAYLOR: Christina said she felt really bad about it, but it wasn't

7   like you'd know she wasn't there.

8 MAGGIE: But I will know!

9 TAYLOR: Only because you're not dead.

10 MAGGIE: So I die and one of my closest friends decides that a

11   biology exam is more important than saying her final

12   good-byes? Well, that's just wonderful! Now I see how

13   important our friendship really was to her!

14 TAYLOR: I wouldn't dwell on it. She really needs to pass this

15   class for her degree.

16 MAGGIE: Well, fine! So tell me, is David all torn up? Is he

17   miserable? Is he confined to bed from the news of my

18   passing? Did they have to give him a sedative to calm him

19   down?

20 TAYLOR: David is being very strong. I just saw him and

21   Christina at Gerardo's.

22 MAGGIE: What? They were at Gerardo's? What were they

23   doing?

24 TAYLOR: Eating.

25 MAGGIE: Eating? How can they eat?

26 TAYLOR: People still get hungry, Maggie.

27 MAGGIE: But ...

28 TAYLOR: Oh, and he was having these fried avocado slices in a

29   sour cream sauce that looked amazing. I'm going to try

30   that next time I'm there.

31 MAGGIE: Excuse me! Does anyone even care that I went

32   swimming in the lake and drowned?

33 TAYLOR: Of course they do, Maggie. But life does go on. And

34   listen, I don't mean to rush you, but I'm meeting Cory at

35   the movies in twenty minutes.

1　MAGGIE: Oh! Well, I'm sorry I had to interrupt your busy
2　　　　schedule to let you know that I'm alive!
3　TAYLOR: It's OK and that's really great news, but can we make
4　　　　this meeting snappy?
5　MAGGIE: Taylor, just do me one favor, OK?
6　TAYLOR: Sure.
7　MAGGIE: Don't tell anyone that you saw me.
8　TAYLOR: OK. So you can make your big entrance at your
9　　　　funeral tomorrow? "Guess what, people? It was a joke! I'm
10　　　　alive!"
11　MAGGIE: No! I'm not coming to my funeral anymore! Instead I
12　　　　think I'll just change my name and my life and start all
13　　　　over. And maybe the next time I pass away my life will be
14　　　　more meaningful to my closest friends.
15　TAYLOR: You're being ridiculous, Maggie.
16　MAGGIE: Oh really? Well then, what about Mitchell? Is he
17　　　　living it up as well? Out dancing tonight to express his
18　　　　sympathy?
19　TAYLOR: Mitchell is another story.
20　MAGGIE: What do you mean?
21　TAYLOR: He is having a hard time.
22　MAGGIE: *(Her face lights up.)* He is?
23　TAYLOR: Uh-huh. He said he hates the idea of attending your
24　　　　funeral. He said he has so many regrets now. So many
25　　　　things he wanted to say to you but didn't.
26　MAGGIE: Really? I wonder what he wanted to tell me?
27　TAYLOR: You can hear it for yourself if you come to your
28　　　　funeral tomorrow.
29　MAGGIE: He's going to speak?
30　TAYLOR: Yes, he is. *(Pulls out a sheet of paper.)* He asked me to
31　　　　look over his eulogy and tell him what I think.
32　MAGGIE: *(Grabs the paper.)* Let me see that!
33　TAYLOR: Hey!
34　MAGGIE: *(Reading)* "Maggie's life was cut too short. Way too
35　　　　short. When I heard the news and I simply could not

1   believe it. Maggie – gone at such a young age. And there
2   were so many things I still wanted to tell her, but didn't
3   have the chance. Of course when I did give her my
4   opinion, she never seemed to listen to me. Oh, if only she
5   had listened to me. If only ... then this incident would have
6   never happened. Well, Maggie, I love you, and I'm sorry I
7   did not have the chance to tell you that."
8   TAYLOR: That's sweet.
9   MAGGIE: "But at this time, I would like to get some things off
10   my chest. As closure for me. Please forgive me for saying
11   this, Maggie, but you are one piece of work!"
12   TAYLOR: *(Tries to grab the paper.)* Maybe you should let me read
13   the rest of this.
14   MAGGIE: No, I can read it!
15   TAYLOR: I'm sure it's just a rough draft.
16   MAGGIE: "Maggie, do the words *it's over* mean anything to
17   you? Or *get out of my face* or *leave me alone!* Tell me? Can
18   you not comprehend what those phrases mean?"
19   TAYLOR: Why is he saying this?
20   MAGGIE: *(Shrugs.)* I don't know.
21   TAYLOR: "Your denial and stubborn determination to win
22   back a man who didn't love you set you on a course of self-
23   destruction. And do I feel sorry for you? Do I? After I told
24   you time and time again to let it go? To stop your pathetic
25   attempts. To let it go once and for all. And did you ever
26   listen to me? No! No siree! Not one single time!"
27   TAYLOR: *(Tries to grab paper.)* Why don't you let me finish
28   reading this?
29   MAGGIE: No! *(Reads on.)* "Think about it. How many times did
30   you cry on my shoulder about wanting David back? The
31   two of you lasted only a few months, but all you could do
32   was obsess over getting him back." *(Looks at TAYLOR.)*
33   Why would he say something like this at my funeral?
34   TAYLOR: Maggie, I think he was just venting. I'm sure he
35   wasn't actually going to say those things. I guess he got

1   tired of always being your shoulder to cry on when he
2   wanted more than that.
3 MAGGIE: Mitchell wanted to be more than my friend?
4 TAYLOR: Maybe you should keep reading.
5 MAGGIE: "And the whole time, I was right there for you. The
6   lunches, the late evening talks, the hugs, the encouraging
7   words ... Could you not see how I felt throughout all of
8   that? That I needed something more than just to be your
9   sounding board? That I cared for you?" *(Gives TAYLOR the*
10   *letter.)* Here, you read the rest of it.
11 TAYLOR: *(Takes letter.)* Are you sure?
12 MAGGIE: Yes.
13 TAYLOR: "I was in love with you, Maggie. Me! The one who was
14   available."
15 MAGGIE: I didn't know that.
16 TAYLOR: "But no! You were obsessed with winning David back.
17   So how did that work out for you?"
18 MAGGIE: It might have worked out had David been a bit more
19   upset that I drowned in the lake!
20 TAYLOR: "All those extreme measures you went to ... and did
21   any of it work? Did it?"
22 MAGGIE: No.
23 TAYLOR: "Buying him a Harley Davidson motorcycle as a
24   present for Flag Day. Really? Who celebrates Flag Day? Did
25   that work?"
26 MAGGIE: No.
27 TAYLOR: "The new wardrobe and hair color. Did that work?"
28 MAGGIE: No.
29 TAYLOR: "Setting up a webpage devoted entirely to your
30   relationship with songs, photos, and endless blogs of your
31   past dates, memories, thoughts, and feelings ... Did that
32   work? No!"
33 MAGGIE: I thought it would.
34 TAYLOR: "The pleading, the begging, the crying, the phone
35   calls ... Did any of that work?"

1   MAGGIE: Obviously not!

2   TAYLOR: "Even when I warned you that you should become

3   the opposite of desperate and needy, did you listen to me?

4   No!"

5   MAGGIE: No.

6   TAYLOR: "And did you listen to me when I said to move on and

7   forget him?"

8   MAGGIE: No.

9   TAYLOR: "Did you listen to me when I said let it go once and for

10   all and stop the scheming, the games, and trying to

11   manipulate him back into your life? Did you? Did you ever

12   listen to me?"

13   MAGGIE: No.

14   TAYLOR: "And we all know your last attempt was a disaster. You

15   made a complete fool of yourself."

16   MAGGIE: Yeah, I know.

17   TAYLOR: I heard about that. You running onto the football

18   field in a bikini holding up a sign asking David to marry

19   you. It got a lot of local airtime, even made it to *Headline*

20   *News,* but no proposal for you.

21   MAGGIE: Go on! Finish reading the stupid eulogy!

22   TAYLOR: *(Reads.)* "And now this?"

23   MAGGIE: What?

24   TAYLOR: "Faking your own death?"

25   MAGGIE: He knows? How could he know?

26   TAYLOR: I imagine because Mitchell knows you better than

27   anyone else. All that time the two of you spent together ...

28   you whining, complaining, crying ... looking for ways to

29   win David back. Maggie, did you ever suggest to Mitchell

30   that you should fake your own death?

31   MAGGIE: I might have, but ...

32   TAYLOR: *(Reading)* "So the last thing that I wish to say to you is

33   this: When your last-ditch effort to win David back blows

34   up in your face, don't come crying to me. Ever again!"

35   MAGGIE: I can't believe this! Mitchell is going to rat me out at

1   my own funeral before I even have the chance to make my
2   grand entrance! How could he do this to me? *(Pause)*
3   Unless he already has. Wait a minute! That's why
4   Christina isn't coming to my funeral, isn't it? She knows
5   I'm not dead! And that's why David's hogging down fried
6   avocados in a sour cream sauce because he also knows I'm
7   not dead! And you know I'm not dead. Heck, I guess the
8   whole world knows I'm not dead. Did you know I wasn't
9   dead when you came to meet me?

10 TAYLOR: I did. I just wanted to see what you had to say.

11 MAGGIE: So my cover was blown a long time ago?

12 TAYLOR: The memorial service was canceled when Mitchell
13   confirmed you were checked into The Ritz Hotel. Sorry.

14 MAGGIE: That's it! I quit! David doesn't care about me and I
15   should just forget about him once and for all!

16 TAYLOR: Oh Maggie, that's so good to hear you say. Really, it's
17   time to quit pursuing him. Some relationships are just not
18   meant to be.

19 MAGGIE: Oh, we were meant to be all right! David just hasn't
20   recognized it yet!

21 TAYLOR: Well, at least now you can recognize that all your
22   scheming did not pay off and it's time to let it go.

23 MAGGIE: But you know, I do have one last plan that might
24   work ... Actually, I'm sure it will!

25 TAYLOR: Maggie, you've got to stop this!

26 MAGGIE: Taylor, I was thinking that if I become famous, then
27   he'll want me for sure, don't you think?

28 TAYLOR: Maggie, I think if buying him a Harley Davidson
29   motorcycle and faking your own death didn't work, I'd say
30   the chances are pretty slim.

31 MAGGIE: No, wait! Listen! What if I become a movie star and I
32   play opposite some of the most handsome men in
33   Hollywood?

34 TAYLOR: Are you telling me that you're going to Hollywood?

35 MAGGIE: I think so ... Yeah!

1 TAYLOR: Are you out of your mind? No, wait! Don't answer
2 that.
3 MAGGIE: Then in a few months, maybe a year, I'll come back to
4 this stupid little town ... in a limo, of course ... and
5 everyone will be gathered around downtown waiting for
6 my arrival. I'll step out of the limo, only to hear my fans,
7 my old friends, screaming my name. All those little people
8 who would have attended my canceled funeral will be
9 screaming out my name. "Maggie! Maggie! Maggie!" And
10 out there will be David ... reaching out, tears streaming
11 down his face ... thrilled to see me again, yet overcome
12 with regret and pain as he realizes that he let me slip
13 through his fingers.
14 TAYLOR: You've got quite the imagination.
15 MAGGIE: Sure, I'll give him a small wave. Then later when he
16 asks for my autograph —
17 TAYLOR: David is going to ask for your autograph?
18 MAGGIE: Yes! Of course he will!
19 TAYLOR: Even after the mounds of letters you wrote to him on
20 a daily basis?
21 MAGGIE: *(Snaps.)* Yes! He's going to ask for my autograph! And
22 I'll say, "Sure, David, I'll give you my autograph. How have
23 you been?" And at that moment he will break down.
24 TAYLOR: He'll break down?
25 MAGGIE: Fall completely apart. *(Demonstrates.)* "Maggie, I've
26 missed you. I've missed you so much! How could I have
27 ever let you go?" And I'll peer over my sunglasses at him
28 and say, "David, it was for the best."
29 TAYLOR: Oh, so you wouldn't jump into his arms at that very
30 moment?
31 MAGGIE: Of course not! After what he's put me through? And
32 then I'll say, "It was nice seeing you again, David. Good-
33 bye." And I'll walk away.
34 TAYLOR: And that's the moment you finally give up on
35 winning him back?

1   MAGGIE: No! Because then he'll start running after me. "Wait,
2   wait! Please wait!" And then he'll ask to take me to dinner
3   while I'm in town. I'll agree, just to be nice, and we'll have
4   dinner, he'll declare his undying love for me, and we'll
5   pick up right where we left off and be married by the end
6   of the year. *(Smiles.)*
7   TAYLOR: You just can't give up on this, can you?
8   MAGGIE: Hollywood, here I come! This is the best plan I've
9   ever come up with! I need to go pack! And you know what?
10   It's probably a good thing that I'm leaving town before too
11   many people see me. Am I dead? Am I alive? We'll just let
12   them figure that out for themselves.
13   TAYLOR: You're unbelievable.
14   MAGGIE: That's probably what they'll say about me in
15   Hollywood. Unbelievable! *(TAYLOR starts to walk off.)* Hey,
16   where are you going?
17   TAYLOR: To meet Cory. We have a movie date, remember?
18   MAGGIE: Well, it won't be long until you'll be seeing me on that
19   big movie screen.
20   TAYLOR: OK. Well, good luck. *(She exits.)*
21   MAGGIE: I don't need luck. I have raw, natural talent. I'll be
22   discovered, become famous, and then everyone will want
23   me ... especially David. *(Looks around.)* A star! That's what
24   I'll be! *(As she exits.)* Hollywood, here I come!
25
26
27
28
29
30
31
32
33
34
35

Drama

13. The Wishing Well

Cast: RACHEL and ALLISON
Setting: Rachel's front porch and front yard

1 RACHEL: Excuse me. Could you please tell me why you are
2   standing on my front porch?
3 ALLISON: I ... uh ...
4 RACHEL: Are you lost?
5 ALLISON: No.
6 RACHEL: Should I call someone for you?
7 ALLISON: No, no. Look, I'm sorry. I guess I should have
8   knocked on your door and asked if I could stand on your
9   porch.
10 RACHEL: And why would you want to stand here on my porch?
11 ALLISON: Because I used to live here.
12 RACHEL: Oh. That must have been a long time ago. I've lived
13   here for ten years.
14 ALLISON: It was a long time ago.
15 RACHEL: So this was your childhood home?
16 ALLISON: Yes. And I wanted to come back and ... I guess just put
17   some things to rest.
18 RACHEL: I see. Well, in that case ...
19 ALLISON: You don't mind if I stand here?
20 RACHEL: No! Not at all. In fact, I wouldn't mind going back to the
21   home where I grew up. It was in Auburn. I drove by there
22   once and it made me feel odd. Part of me felt like I could
23   jump out of the car and rush into the house, and the other
24   part of me felt almost betrayed as I looked at the unfamiliar
25   lawn furniture and vehicles in the driveway. Is that how you
26   feel? As if I'm the intruder?

1 ALLISON: *(Smiles.)* No, not really. I just wanted to remember
2   some things. The good things.
3 RACHEL: I see. *(Offers her hand.)* I'm Rachel.
4 ALLISON: I'm Allison. Thank you for being so understanding.
5 RACHEL: Absolutely. So, you were happy growing up here?
6 ALLISON: Yes. *(Smiles.)* My best friend lived right across the
7   street. *(Points.)* Right there.
8 RACHEL: What was her name?
9 ALLISON: Becky. She and I used to ride our bikes all over the
10   neighborhood. Over to Tim's, to Maggie's, down to the
11   corner store ... Sometimes we'd make a sack lunch and
12   take it to the school and sit on the front steps and talk
13   about everything imaginable. It was the best time of my
14   life!
15 RACHEL: I guess your friend Becky moved away, too?
16 ALLISON: Yes. We both moved.
17 RACHEL: Peter and April live across the street now. Nice young
18   couple.
19 ALLISON: I don't know where Becky is now. We lost touch.
20 RACHEL: That's a shame. Especially with the two of you being
21   best friends. So, tell me, does the neighborhood look
22   different from when you grew up here?
23 ALLISON: Yes. Becky's house used to be white. Now it's bright
24   blue.
25 RACHEL: Can't say I like it.
26 ALLISON: Me neither.
27 RACHEL: And my house ... well, your house, used to have
28   honeysuckle bushes under the front windows.
29 ALLISON: Really? I like honeysuckle. They weren't here when
30   we moved in.
31 RACHEL: And we used to have a wishing well in the yard.
32 RACHEL: A wishing well?
33 ALLISON: *(Points.)* Right over there.
34 RACHEL: It wasn't here when Patrick and I moved in. All we
35   had were weeds. Took us months to get rid of them. A

1   wishing well, huh? You don't see those nowadays.

2   ALLISON: No. And of course it wasn't real. It was just a

3   decorative piece in the yard. But Becky and I would

4   pretend it was real.

5   RACHEL: So the two of you would make wishes?

6   ALLISON: *(Smiling as she recalls)* Oh, yes! And most of them

7   were ridiculous. You know, like, I wish Mike Jenkins

8   would ask me out. Or I wish summer would last forever.

9   And then later, I wished ... *(Stops herself.)*

10   RACHEL: What?

11   ALLISON: Nothing.

12   RACHEL: Let me guess. You wished for a million dollars!

13   ALLISON: I probably wished that, too ... but that's not what I

14   was remembering.

15   RACHEL: What? What did your wish for?

16   ALLISON: I wished that something bad hadn't happened.

17   RACHEL: Something bad happened?

18   ALLISON: Yes. Something so bad that it changed everything. It

19   changed my life, Becky's life, and everyone's around us.

20   RACHEL: Oh! Did someone die?

21   ALLISON: No, no one died. Except for maybe our spirits.

22   RACHEL: I'm sorry.

23   ALLISON: But before that, life was grand. Becky and I had so

24   much fun. So much energy. So many ideas. Once we

25   collected horny toads and sold them for a dollar apiece. I

26   think we made four dollars. *(Laughs.)* And I remember

27   when we tied thread around the necks of locusts and flew

28   them like kites. And we planted cotton in the alley. And

29   ran through the sprinklers. Jumped off the roof onto

30   Becky's trampoline. Oh, we had so much fun. *(Short

31   pause)* And then it all ended.

32   RACHEL: Would you like to come inside? I could make us some

33   iced tea.

34   ALLISON: No, that's all right.

35   RACHEL: Are you sure? It's quite warm outside today.

1   **ALLISON:** Thank you, but I'm sure. *(Looks around.)* **I realize the**
2   **neighborhood doesn't look the same, but as I stand here**
3   **on your front porch, it feels as if I could turn around and**
4   **go inside and everything would be the same. I'd like that.**
5   **RACHEL: I understand. And you can stay here as long as you'd**
6   **like. Patrick and I enjoy sitting out here. And it's nice to**
7   **meet someone who used to live in our house. And who**
8   **used to run up and down the streets, laughing with her**
9   **best friend, and making wishes in the wishing well. You**
10   **know, I wish that wishing well were still in the yard.**
11   **ALLISON: Me too. Becky and I would even drop coins into that**
12   **little well. Of course we always caught my brother fishing**
13   **them out when he thought we weren't looking. Then**
14   **when he had enough money saved, he'd run down to the**
15   **store and buy a package of balloons.**
16   **RACHEL: You're brother liked balloons?**
17   **ALLISON: Yes, but only if they were filled with water.**
18   **RACHEL:** *(Laughs.)* **I see.**
19   **ALLISON: Ricky ... that was my brother's name, well, he would**
20   **hide around that corner over there with his ammunition**
21   **of colored water balloons. Patiently waiting. Then as**
22   **Becky and I walked by, suddenly out of nowhere,** *splat!*
23   **RACHEL: Oh, no! I remember doing that as a kid.**
24   **ALLISON: Becky and I would scream and run away as fast as we**
25   **could. But here would come my brother, a water balloon**
26   **in each hand, chasing us until he caught us. He usually**
27   **soaked us pretty good.**
28   **RACHEL: That must have been fun.**
29   **ALLISON: It was. It was all fun. I just wish ...** *(Stops herself.)*
30   **RACHEL: You wish you still had your wishing well, don't you?**
31   *(ALLISON nods.)* **Well, maybe you could pretend.**
32   **ALLISON: Pretend?**
33   **RACHEL: Yes. Pretend your wishing well is still in the yard.**
34   **ALLISON: It won't change anything.**
35   **RACHEL: But if it could?**

1   **ALLISON: What would I wish?** *(Takes a breath. Short pause)* **I'd**
2   **wish that I could go back and change things.**
3   **RACHEL: What things?**
4   **ALLISON: Rewrite history, I suppose. That's some big wish,**
5   **isn't it? But this time, Becky and I are riding our bikes**
6   **home from the store, just like we were that day. And we**
7   **fall onto the green grass under the shade tree, catching**
8   **our breath, and laughing as we dig into our sacks of**
9   **candy, hoping my brother is not around the corner with**
10   **plans to soak us. No one gets upset. No one cries. Becky is**
11   **not sent home and I'm not made to go inside the house.**
12   **RACHEL: Did you two girls get into some sort of trouble?**
13   **ALLISON: No, but it felt that way.**
14   **RACHEL: And that's the day everything changed?**
15   **ALLISON: Yes.** *(Steps forward.)* **You know, I am going to pretend**
16   **that wishing well is still here.**
17   **RACHEL: What did it look like?**
18   **ALLISON: It was this round, red-bricked well with a little roof**
19   **on top of it. And I would kneel down** *(Gets on her knees)*
20   **and I would drop a penny into the well and make a wish.**
21   **RACHEL: You should do that.**
22   **ALLISON:** *(Closes eyes.)* **I wish I could go back. Back to the time**
23   **before everything changed. And I wish I could open my**
24   **eyes and see Becky waving at me from across the street.**
25   **Her dark hair pulled back into a ponytail. The hot pink**
26   **shoelaces in her tennis shoes. Her running across the**
27   **street so we can jump on our bikes and take off. And**
28   **everything would be the same. And it would be like that**
29   **forever. That's what I wish for.** *(Opens her eyes.)*
30   **RACHEL:** *(After a pause)* **So what happened, Allison?**
31   **ALLISON:** *(Stands.)* **What happened? My mother caught my dad**
32   **with Becky's mom.**
33   **RACHEL: Oh, I'm sorry!**
34   **ALLISON: And that's when everything changed. My parents**
35   **divorced. Her parents divorced. Everyone moved. Becky**

1   blamed my dad. I blamed her mom.

2 RACHEL: And you never saw Becky again?

3 ALLISON: No. I don't know what happened to her. Or where she

4   moved.

5 RACHEL: So your dad and Becky's mom ... did they marry?

6 ALLISON: No. But everyone split up and went in different

7   directions.

8 RACHEL: That's so sad, Allison. I'm sure you wonder what

9   happened to your best friend.

10 ALLISON: All the time. I would do anything to see her again.

11   But I don't think that'll ever happen.

12 RACHEL: I'm sure Becky misses you, too.

13 ALLISON: Maybe. I don't know. There's no way of knowing. And

14   like I said, I have no idea where she moved.

15 RACHEL: Have you searched for her online?

16 ALLISON: Yes, but nothing ever came up. *(Glances up.)* She

17   always planned to go to the moon. She was going to

18   become an astronaut. Of course she'd say this when we

19   were lying on a blanket in the grass looking up at the sky.

20   She also said she wanted to live here forever. And after she

21   went to the moon she might become a teacher. Thought

22   she'd be a teacher at our old school down the street.

23 RACHEL: Maybe she did become a teacher.

24 ALLISON: Maybe. And Becky had this one favorite saying.

25   "Forever is composed of nows."

26 RACHEL: Emily Dickinson!

27 ALLISON: How did you know?

28 RACHEL: My son's English teacher ... Peter's teacher has that

29   quote above her desk. You don't suppose ... ?

30 ALLISON: Of course not. She moved off.

31 RACHEL: But you said she wanted to live here forever and

32   teach at the school.

33 ALLISON: And I wanted to live here forever, too.

34 RACHEL: Well, I don't recall Peter's English teacher's first

35   name, but her name is Miss Henson.

1   ALLISON: What?

2   RACHEL: Miss Henson. She's Paul's seventh grade English

3   teacher. He really likes her, too. And believe it or not, my

4   thirteen-year-old son has even learned to appreciate

5   poetry. Yes, Emily Dickinson, Edgar Allan Poe, Robert

6   Frost.

7   ALLISON: Have you met her?

8   RACHEL: Yes. I met her at open house. She hardly seems old

9   enough to be teaching. I'd say she's close to your age.

10   ALLISON: Does she have brown hair?

11   RACHEL: Yes, she does.

12   ALLISON: And does she have this little scar on her chin?

13   RACHEL: A scar? I don't remember. But I do remember her

14   eyes. Very big brown eyes.

15   ALLISON: Like the moon?

16   RACHEL: Oh, Allison. Do you think it might be Becky?

17   ALLISON: Becky Henson had brown eyes as big as the moon!

18   RACHEL: And her last name was Henson?

19   ALLISON: Yes. Becky Henson who was obsessed with poetry.

20   Especially Emily Dickinson. And she loved that quote so

21   much that she wrote it on her bedroom wall. "Forever is

22   composed of nows."

23   RACHEL: It doesn't sound like a coincidence.

24   ALLISON: And Becky Henson who lived across the street from

25   me said she'd never leave this town.

26   RACHEL: Then maybe she came back.

27   ALLISON: When does school let out?

28   RACHEL: *(Looks at watch.)* In thirty minutes.

29   ALLISON: Thank you!

30   RACHEL: Are you going to the school?

31   ALLISON: Yes!

32   RACHEL: And do you really think it's Becky?

33   ALLISON: I'm sure it is!

34   RACHEL: And do you think you'll be able to mend the hurts

35   from your past?

1 **ALLISON: I don't know. But I sure hope so.**

2 **RACHEL: You know, Allison, maybe you should make one last**

3   **wish.**

4 **ALLISON: Yes. Yes, I think I will!** *(Steps forward and kneels*

5   *down.)* **I no longer wish to go back, but to go forward. I**

6   **wish to open my eyes and find my best friend. And I wish**

7   **the past will draw us close, but not hold us back. And I**

8   **wish ... I wish that our nows become forever.**

9

10

11

12

13

14

15

16

17

18

19

20

21

22

23

24

25

26

27

28

29

30

31

32

33

34

35

14. Snap

Cast: VICTORIA and MARICELA
Setting: Maricela's bedroom

1   **VICTORIA: Maricela.**

2   **MARICELA: Yeah?**

3   **VICTORIA: Have you ever wondered what causes people to**
4   **snap?**

5   **MARICELA: Snap? As in lose control and do something you**
6   **regret later?**

7   **VICTORIA: Yeah. Like this terrible thought crosses your mind**
8   **and for a moment you consider doing it.**

9   **MARICELA: Like what?**

10   **VICTORIA: Like grabbing a sharp object and ...**

11   **MARICELA: And hurting someone?**

12   **VICTORIA: Maybe.**

13   **MARICELA: Victoria, everyone has random thoughts like that**
14   **for a couple of seconds, but who follows through with it?**
15   **Except for maybe the mentally deranged people, but those**
16   **incidents are rare.**

17   **VICTORIA: But I'm just wondering at what point does the**
18   **thought become more than just a thought?**

19   **MARICELA: What are you talking about?**

20   **VICTORIA: Have you ever wanted to kill someone?**

21   **MARICELA: Sure.**

22   **VICTORIA: Who?**

23   **MARICELA: Uh, my little brother, Tim. Like last Saturday he**
24   **snuck into my room and borrowed my makeup for his**
25   **artwork. Oh, I was so mad! So picture this, red**
26   **construction paper with a weird looking house, trees,**

1   fluffy clouds, and a big rainbow across the top. All drawn
2   with my makeup! Yeah, I wanted to kill that little brat!
3   VICTORIA: Maricela, I'm serious.
4   MARICELA: OK, what are you talking about? You want
5   someone to die?
6   VICTORIA: Sometimes.
7   MARICELA: Who?
8   VICTORIA: A person who's supposed to love me and protect
9   me.
10   MARICELA: Sounds like a parent to me.
11   VICTORIA: It's my mom.
12   MARICELA: Your mom? Are you serious?
13   VICTORIA: Have you ever felt that way?
14   MARICELA: That I want my mom to die? No! I mean,
15   sometimes I get mad at her, but I don't want her to walk
16   out in front of a bus or get some awful news from the
17   doctor. And why would you even say something like that
18   about your mom?
19   VICTORIA: Never mind. Just never mind, OK?
20   MARICELA: No, tell me! Tell me, Victoria!
21   VICTORIA: Because for once I'd like to come home and have
22   my mother greet me with a smile. Ask how my day was.
23   Ask when the next choir concert is. And actually go to it!
24   Maricela, do you know what it's like to stand on the risers
25   on that hot stage and realize that you're the only choir
26   member who doesn't have a single person there to listen
27   to you?
28   MARICELA: Your mom doesn't go to your choir concerts?
29   VICTORIA: No. And you know what I do?
30   MARICELA: What?
31   VICTORIA: I look out into the audience and pick out a smiling
32   mother and pretend she's mine. Isn't that stupid?
33   MARICELA: Victoria, what's wrong with your mother? Why
34   doesn't she go to your concerts? Is she sick?
35   VICTORIA: I think some people call it a disease.

1   MARICELA: What's wrong with her?

2   VICTORIA: She's a drunk! That's what's wrong with her!

3   MARICELA: Your mom's an alcoholic?

4   VICTORIA: I prefer to call her a drunk. An alcoholic sounds like

5   something that can be cured. My mom can't be cured.

6   MARICELA: How do you know that? She could go to Alcoholics

7   Anonymous.

8   VICTORIA: And who's going to make her go? Me?

9   MARICELA: Well, you could suggest ...

10 VICTORIA: *(Laughs.)* Sure, sure. But do I suggest the AA

11   meetings when she's passed out drunk or when she's

12   having another episode of nonsense rage? *(Laughs.)* I can

13   just hear it now. "Mom, wake up! Wake up! Change out of

14   that robe and house shoes so I can drive you to an AA

15   meeting! What? You haven't showered in a few days?

16   That's OK. No one will notice." Or how about this? "Mom,

17   please stop screaming and listen to me! Listen! OK, if it

18   makes you feel better to turn the furniture over, then go

19   ahead. But listen, Mom, I want you to calm down so I can

20   drive you to an AA meeting. What? You'd rather throw the

21   dishes at me? Stop it, Mom! Stop it!"

22 MARICELA: Victoria, I'm so sorry. I didn't know your mother

23   had a problem with alcohol.

24 VICTORIA: That's because no one ever comes to my house.

25 MARICELA: My cousin Mike used to have a problem with

26   drinking.

27 VICTORIA: What happened?

28 MARICELA: He went to jail. Twice.

29 VICTORIA: And now?

30 MARICELA: He finally sobered up. But not in time to save his

31   marriage.

32 VICTORIA: Yeah? Well, I'd like for my mom to go to jail. I know!

33   Maybe I could shove her into the car while she's plastered

34   and suggest she go do a little shopping. Think that'd work?

35 MARICELA: Sure, I think she'd get arrested, but what if she

1   killed someone on the way?

2 VICTORIA: True. I wouldn't want that to happen. I wouldn't

3   want an innocent person to get hurt because of my

4   mother. But sometimes ... sometimes I wouldn't care if her

5   car plummeted right off a bridge!

6 MARICELA: Victoria, you shouldn't say things like that!

7 VICTORIA: Or think those things either, right? That's my

8   problem. I'm afraid that one day I'm going to walk into my

9   house after a really bad day and then I'm going to snap.

10 MARICELA: You wouldn't do that.

11 VICTORIA: How do you know? What if I'm feeling worse than I

12   did a couple of nights ago? And there I am in the kitchen

13   cutting up an apple and she starts screaming at me again.

14   But this time, instead of getting mad and slamming the

15   knife into the sink, I walk into the living room and ... and ...

16 MARICELA: Victoria!

17 VICTORIA: Who's to say I wouldn't snap? You don't know.

18 MARICELA: Because if you stop and think about it for a

19   minute, you realize that an act like that would send you

20   straight to jail. And you wouldn't want that. Would you?

21 VICTORIA: No. But when people commit a crime, do they

22   actually stop and think about things like that? Going to

23   jail? Or are they just living in the moment? Perhaps an

24   unbearable moment? And all the rational thoughts are

25   drowned out by the pain and anger they are feeling.

26 MARICELA: I don't know, Victoria, but you don't want to find

27   out. Instead, maybe you could try something else.

28 VICTORIA: Like what?

29 MARICELA: Why don't you pour all the liquor down the drain?

30 VICTORIA: *(Halfhearted laugh)* Yeah, that's a good idea. I

31   wonder how many empty liquor bottles would fly at my

32   head while I'm doing that?

33 MARICELA: Pour it out and then lock yourself in your room so

34   she can't come in.

35 VICTORIA: Sure. And then she'll bang on my door in an

1   uncontrollable fit of rage. And if I don't come out, she'll
2   rip the door completely off its hinges. So you see, I'm
3   stuck. Stuck in the house with a mad alcoholic who will
4   never be a mother to me!
5 MARICELA: But if you poured it all out —
6 VICTORIA: If I poured it all out? If I poured it all out she'd just
7   walk down the road to the liquor store and buy more
8   booze!
9 MARICELA: I know! Why don't you call Child Protective
10   Services on her?
11 VICTORIA: And do what? Move into a foster home? No! I don't
12   want to do that! Besides, I'm not a child.
13 MARICELA: You're not an adult either. It's better than living in
14   the nightmare you are describing.
15 VICTORIA: I can't.
16 MARICELA: I thought you wanted to get away?
17 VICTORIA: I do, but ... it's complicated. Who's going to take care
18   of her?
19 MARICELA: Victoria, a minute ago you were afraid you might
20   lose control and do something bad to your own mother!
21   And now you're worried about her being left alone?
22 VICTORIA: Maricela, you don't understand!
23 MARICELA: I'm trying to understand, Victoria!
24 VICTORIA: I know. I just want her to be that smiling face at my
25   choir concert.
26 MARICELA: I understand that. And you need to understand
27   that your mother needs help. You've got to find a way to
28   see that she gets the support she needs.
29 VICTORIA: How?
30 MARICELA: I'm not sure. But if we talked to Mrs. Riggs at
31   school —
32 VICTORIA: No! I don't want to do that!
33 MARICELA: Victoria, it's a step in the right direction. And
34   that's what you *and* your mother need.
35 VICTORIA: I know, but —

1　MARICELA: Victoria, something has to be done!
2　VICTORIA: I know. That's all I've been thinking about since last
3　　　night.
4　MARICELA: What happened last night?
5　VICTORIA: I was in my room. It was after midnight and I'd
6　　　fallen asleep while studying for a history test. Then all of
7　　　a sudden I woke up to my mom dragging me out of the bed
8　　　by my ankles.
9　MARICELA: Why did she do that?
10　VICTORIA: She wanted me to get up and clean the kitchen.
11　MARICELA: In the middle of the night?
12　VICTORIA: Yes.
13　MARICELA: So what did you do?
14　VICTORIA: Well, at first I screamed at her. I told her to stop.
15　MARICELA: Did she?
16　VICTORIA: No.
17　MARICELA: So what did you do?
18　VICTORIA: What I always do. I did what she said so she'd stop.
19　　　I got up, went into the kitchen and started washing the
20　　　dishes. That is, until she passed out again. Then I went
21　　　back to bed.
22　MARICELA: Victoria, you've got to get out of that house!
23　VICTORIA: Easier said than done.
24　MARICELA: What about staying with a relative?
25　VICTORIA: My closest relative, Aunt Eileen, lives five states
26　　　over. And she doesn't care.
27　MARICELA: Your dad?
28　VICTORIA: I haven't seen him since I was five.
29　MARICELA: I have an idea.
30　VICTORIA: What?
31　MARICELA: You can stay with me at my house. I'm sure my
32　　　parents won't mind. Especially under the circumstances.
33　　　And there's plenty of room. And that would give you time
34　　　to figure out what to do.
35　VICTORIA: Thanks, Maricela, but I don't think so.

1   MARICELA: Victoria, it's a perfect solution! We can go to my
2   house after school and talk to my parents about it. Do you
3   need to stop by your house and get some things? I can go
4   with you.
5   VICTORIA: Maricela, you don't understand. I can't leave her.
6   MARICELA: Why not?
7   VICTORIA: Because I have to take care of her. No one else is
8   going to.
9   MARICELA: Victoria, she can take care of herself!
10 VICTORIA: No she can't! Who do you think buys the food? Sees
11   that her prescriptions are filled? Cleans the house? Takes
12   out the trash? Waters the plants? I do everything!
13 MARICELA: Then make sure she has what she needs and then
14   leave! The trash can pile up and the plants can die!
15   Victoria, it's better than the alternative.
16 VICTORIA: Well, you know how it looks to me?
17 MARICELA: How?
18 VICTORIA: Like either way it's a no-win situation.
19 MARICELA: Maybe so, but you don't need to stay there and
20   watch her drink herself to death!
21 VICTORIA: I know it doesn't make any sense to you, Maricela,
22   but I can't leave her. I just can't.
23 MARICELA: Then what are you going to do? Because you
24   yourself said that if you stay you might snap.
25 VICTORIA: I know. And I don't want to. I'm trying not to. But
26   sometimes I'm just afraid.
27 MARICELA: Then maybe you should tell someone. Someone
28   besides me. An adult.
29 VICTORIA: *(Shakes her head.)* No! I can't! So just forget I ever
30   told you this, OK?
31 MARICELA: Forget what you told me? How can I forget what
32   you just told me? You're living in a nightmare! Your mom
33   is a drunk who's out of control and to top it off, you feel as
34   if you've reached your breaking point. How can I forget
35   something like that?

1   **VICTORIA:** Maricela, you better not tell anyone what I told you!

2   **MARICELA:** Victoria, someone needs to say something!

3   **VICTORIA:** No! Forget it! I was just rambling! I don't even know

4   what I was talking about! It's not really that bad. I mean,

5   not all the time. Look, you misunderstood what I was

6   trying to say. Like last night when she wanted me to clean

7   the kitchen —

8   **MARICELA:** When she drug you out of the bed by your ankles?

9   **VICTORIA:** Because it was my fault! I'm the one who decided to

10   cook spaghetti for dinner! I'm the one who splattered

11   spaghetti sauce all over the stove! And I knew the rules

12   about cleaning up the kitchen after I cooked! It was my

13   fault she got mad!

14 **MARICELA:** Oh, and dragging you out of the bed by your ankles

15   while you're sleeping is justified? Victoria, don't you think

16   any other mom would have waited until the next morning

17   to remind you of the rules? Or even ground you if that was

18   needed? But what she did was insane!

19 **VICTORIA:** You don't understand! She just has these rules! And

20   I knew those rules! I knew better than to cook and not

21   clean up my mess afterwards.

22 **MARICELA:** And when was the last time she cooked for you?

23   *(Pause)* Or cleaned the house? *(Pause)* Or went to your

24   choir concert or any other activity you were in? *(Pause)*

25 **VICTORIA:** She's not well.

26 **MARICELA:** Not well? Victoria, she's an alcoholic!

27 **VICTORIA:** Shut up, Maricela! Not everyone can have a perfect

28   family like you!

29 **MARICELA:** My family is not perfect, Victoria! But I'm not

30   pushed to the point where I want to hurt someone I love.

31 **VICTORIA:** I was being dramatic, OK? Just like when you got

32   mad at Tim for drawing with your makeup.

33 **MARICELA:** It's not the same thing and you know it! I wouldn't go

34   cut an apple and think, "Gosh, maybe instead I'll just go into

35   the living room and shove the knife in Tim."

1 VICTORIA: Shut up, Maricela! It wasn't like that!

2 MARICELA: Then what was it like? Huh? What was it like?

3 VICTORIA: *(Screams.)* I don't know! I mean ... I wanted ... for a

4   minute ... maybe more than a minute ...

5 MARICELA: What? Tell me!

6 VICTORIA: I want it to end! That's all I want! I just wanted it to

7   end! *(Pause)* But it never will end. Never. And I'll never

8   have a mother at my choir concert. Ever.

9 MARICELA: I'm so sorry.

10 VICTORIA: Forget it.

11 MARICELA: Victoria ...

12 VICTORIA: Yeah?

13 MARICELA: Come on. Let's go.

14 VICTORIA: Where?

15 MARICELA: To talk to Mrs. Riggs.

16 VICTORIA: The school counselor?

17 MARICELA: It'll be good. I'll go with you. She's really nice, you

18   know.

19 VICTORIA: I don't know, Maricela ...

20 MARICELA: Come on. You can do this.

21

22

23

24

25

26

27

28

29

30

31

32

33

34

35

15. Night Storm

Cast: BETH and FRANKIE
Setting: Bathroom of a convenience store

1　FRANKIE: Do you think we're safe in here?

2　BETH: I think we're safer in here than out there.

3　FRANKIE: Have you ever been in a tornado before?

4　BETH: Once. It ripped some shingles off my house in Wichita.
5　　　　I think we just caught the edge of it. But I have seen the
6　　　　damage a tornado can do. A massive one ripped through
7　　　　my grandparents' community and devastated the area.
8　　　　Obliterated homes, uprooted trees, threw cars across the
9　　　　road ... I'd never seen anything like it.

10　FRANKIE: What about your grandparents? Were they OK?

11　BETH: They were in the cellar. Thank God. Because if they
12　　　　hadn't been ...

13　FRANKIE: What about us? Are you sure this is the best place for
14　　　　us to be?

15　BETH: I think for a convenience store with an entire wall of
16　　　　glass, the restroom is our best choice. We'll be fine.

17　FRANKIE: I hope so, because I don't want to die. I'm only
18　　　　nineteen.

19　BETH: We aren't going to die. I'm Beth, by the way.

20　FRANKIE: I'm Frankie.

21　BETH: So, Frankie, who's all but nineteen-years-old, they let
22　　　　you work at this convenience store all alone in the middle
23　　　　of the night?

24　FRANKIE: I get paid extra to work this shift. Not too many
25　　　　people like working at three a.m. Do you work nights, too?

26　BETH: Oh no. I don't work.

1 FRANKIE: But you like to stay up late?

2 BETH: I couldn't sleep. Decided to run up the street for a cup of

3   coffee.

4 FRANKIE: Coffee when you can't sleep?

5 BETH: I didn't think I'd be able to get back to sleep, so ... why

6   not?

7 FRANKIE: Good point. Listen! Do you hear that?

8 BETH: *(Nods.)* Yes. It's hailing now.

9 FRANKIE: Should we look out?

10 BETH: I think we better keep the door shut until the sirens stop

11   blaring.

12 FRANKIE: You know, on those nice sunny days when I hear

13   those sirens go off, I never give it a second thought. I know

14   it's only a test. But now, this is the real thing!

15 BETH: I know. It is frightening when you know the sirens are

16   blaring for a reason.

17 FRANKIE: I should've grabbed the radio.

18 BETH: When the storm calms down, we'll get the radio and see

19   what's going on. For now I think we should stay put.

20 FRANKIE: All right.

21 BETH: And in the meantime, why don't we talk about

22   something to get our minds off the storm?

23 FRANKIE: That's going to be hard with all the horrible sounds.

24   The wind howling, the hail beating down on the roof, the

25   front door banging back and forth. Not to mention those

26   sirens. But if you want, I guess we can try.

27 BETH: OK, I have a question for you.

28 FRANKIE: What's that?

29 BETH: Why is it that all convenience stores have such filthy

30   restrooms?

31 FRANKIE: Really? That's what you want to know?

32 BETH: I do. They're all unsanitary. Toilets don't work. Floors

33   are dirty and stained. Cigarette butts thrown in the sink.

34   Obscenities scrawled on the walls. I just don't get it. Do

35   you never clean them?

1 FRANKIE: Well, I don't. I work the night shift and I'm the only
2   person here. I figured the day people took care of it.
3 BETH: It doesn't appear that they do. And there's another point
4   I'd like to make. There are never any paper towels. The
5   holder is always empty. Why is that?
6 FRANKIE: We don't offer paper towels anymore. Now it's the
7   earth-friendly hot air.
8 BETH: I hate that.
9 FRANKIE: Me too.
10 BETH: And honestly, it stinks in here.
11 FRANKIE: I know. And I think it'd be sad to die in a smelly
12   bathroom, don't you?
13 BETH: We're not going to die. So, Frankie, do you attend
14   college?
15 FRANKIE: No. But I'm hoping to go next semester. Money's
16   been a little tight for me.
17 BETH: Do you have family to help?
18 FRANKIE: No.
19 BETH: No?
20 FRANKIE: It's complicated.
21 BETH: I'm sorry.
22 FRANKIE: Did you go to school?
23 BETH: Yes. I graduated with a degree in communications. I
24   wanted to be a news anchor.
25 FRANKIE: What happened?
26 BETH: Well, I married a man who wanted a stay-at-home wife.
27   Money wasn't an issue for us, and Ted, that was my
28   husband, he was quite insistent on me being around for
29   him. He didn't like the idea of coming home to an empty
30   house. So, that's what I did.
31 FRANKIE: That's nice not having to worry about money. It's
32   always been an issue for me.
33 BETH: Always been an issue for you? You're only nineteen.
34 FRANKIE: I've been on my own for a while. Like I said, it's
35   complicated. But if you don't have to worry about making

1   rent or paying the electric bill or having enough money
2   left over for food, *wow!* You're lucky.
3 BETH: Lucky?
4 FRANKIE: Yeah! I can't even imagine what that'd be like.
5 BETH: Well, I don't feel very lucky.
6 FRANKIE: Why not?
7 BETH: I could say it's complicated as well. Ted, my husband, he
8   walked out on me a few months ago.
9 FRANKIE: Why?
10 BETH: For another woman. Actually, I'd say for a kid. I think
11   she's about your age.
12 FRANKIE: I'm sorry.
13 BETH: I was too, but now, *(Shrugs)* good riddance. I never did
14   like his snoring. Or the way he rattled the newspaper
15   when he read it. Or the way he screamed at the football
16   players on TV. So I think I'm better off.
17 FRANKIE: That's good that you feel that way.
18 BETH: But the nights ... they seem long. I'm not used to
19   sleeping alone.
20 FRANKIE: Is that why you can't sleep?
21 BETH: Maybe. Or maybe it's a million things running through
22   my mind. What am I going to do with my life? There has to
23   be something out there for me.
24 FRANKIE: Maybe you should get a job.
25 BETH: I think you're right. *(Small laugh)* Maybe I'd like your
26   job.
27 FRANKIE: Oh no! You wouldn't like my job!
28 BETH: A job is what you make of it. I think you could find
29   satisfaction in almost anything. Even cleaning
30   bathrooms. And I would definitely clean this bathroom.
31   And set out some paper towels.
32 FRANKIE: My boss wouldn't let you do that.
33 BETH: What? Work here?
34 FRANKIE: No. Set out paper towels. He's in this earth-friendly,
35   go green mode.

1   **BETH:** I just haven't got into that whole recycle thing. Does that
2   make me a bad person?
3   **FRANKIE:** No. At least I don't think so. So, what do you do? I
4   mean, with your free time?
5   **BETH:** What do I do? Well, I'm a member of the Junior
6   Women's Club.
7   **FRANKIE:** What's that about?
8   **BETH:** Well, it's designed to bring women together who have a
9   shared interest in the arts, public affairs, education,
10   community service –
11   **FRANKIE:** That sounds boring.
12   **BETH:** *(Smiles.)* Sometimes it is.
13   **FRANKIE:** Is that all you do?
14   **BETH:** Well, I shop.
15   **FRANKIE:** You shop?
16   **BETH:** I like to buy things. Mostly for my house. You know,
17   decorate. Shop for unique pieces of art that fit my style.
18   **FRANKIE:** What is your style?
19   **BETH:** Modern. No. More contemporary. Well, actually I like
20   antiques.
21   **FRANKIE:** Sounds like you like a little bit of everything.
22   **BETH:** Yes, that's it.
23   **FRANKIE:** No kids?
24   **BETH:** No.
25   **FRANKIE:** Do you get lonely?
26   **BETH:** Lonely? Sometimes. I'm just not satisfied with my life
27   right now, you know? I need some direction. Some goals.
28   Some dreams.
29   **FRANKIE:** Oh, I've got plenty of dreams! I just need to find a
30   way to reach them.
31   **BETH:** And what is it you want, Frankie?
32   **FRANKIE:** I want to sing! It's my passion.
33   **BETH:** Really?
34   **FRANKIE:** Yes. I've been singing since the day I learned to talk.
35   Sometimes when there are no customers in the store,

1   which happens a lot between the hours of two and four in
2   the morning, I sing at the top of my lungs. *(She laughs at*
3   *herself.)*
4   BETH: A singer, huh?
5   FRANKIE: Yeah.
6   BETH: What type of music do you like?
7   FRANKIE: Just about everything. But I lean toward
8   contemporary. I like Nora Jones. Have you heard of her?
9   BETH: I have.
10   FRANKIE: Someday I'd like to take off to New York or LA and
11   see if I can break into the music industry.
12   BETH: That's a mighty big dream.
13   FRANKIE: I know.
14   BETH: And it's great, but just be careful not to set your
15   aspirations too high.
16   FRANKIE: Why's that?
17   BETH: So early on you don't get disappointed or discouraged.
18   Start out with a smaller dream and move up from there.
19   FRANKIE: So what do I do?
20   BETH: How about getting hooked up with a local band? Or start
21   your own band if that's what it takes.
22   FRANKIE: That's not a bad idea. Can you sing? Maybe you could
23   be in my band.
24   BETH: Me? Oh no. I can't carry a tune. *(They share a laugh.)* And
25   come to think of it, my friend Eddie, he's always a big
26   sponsor at our women's fundraisers, owns a piano bar
27   downtown. Maybe I could speak to him about you singing
28   there.
29   FRANKIE: You'd do that? But you don't even know me!
30   BETH: I think after being stuck with you in a filthy
31   convenience store bathroom in the middle of the night,
32   we've become great friends, don't you think?
33   FRANKIE: *(Smiles.)* I do!
34   BETH: It still sounds pretty bad out there.
35   FRANKIE: I think it's getting worse. And I really don't want to

1   die tonight if I might have the chance to sing at a piano

2   bar.

3   BETH: You'll get your chance. And I'll come hear you sing, all

4   right?

5   FRANKIE: You would?

6   BETH: I would.

7   FRANKIE: You know what? Maybe I could set something up for

8   you, too.

9   BETH: What's that?

10   FRANKIE: Well, you wanted to be a news anchor, right?

11   BETH: And you have some connections for me?

12   FRANKIE: Actually, I do. The Channel Nine manager comes

13   into the store every night for coffee after their final

14   newscast. I'll give him your number and tell him to give

15   you a call.

16   BETH: *(Laughs.)* Oh, like he would do that!

17   FRANKIE: He would call you!

18   BETH: Oh, to be young and have such faith! Sweetheart, they

19   hire seasoned pros, not someone like me who's been

20   attending women's meetings and shopping for the last ten

21   years.

22   FRANKIE: Well, you may have to start out with a smaller

23   dream. Just like you told me.

24   BETH: What do you mean?

25   FRANKIE: Channel Nine is looking for a part-time receptionist.

26   Mr. Mack offered me the job, but I couldn't do it with my

27   nighttime schedule. But if you took the job, maybe you

28   could move up from part-time receptionist to full-time

29   receptionist to camera operator to news anchor.

30   BETH: A part-time receptionist, huh? That sounds interesting.

31   I mean, I'd love to work at a news station. And I suppose

32   it's possible I could work myself up to a better job.

33   FRANKIE: Mr. Mack told me to let him know if I knew of

34   anyone looking for a job. And you're the first person I

35   know who's looking for a job. And how perfect is that?

1   BETH: It does sound perfect.

2   FRANKIE: It is. *(Grabs BETH's arm.)* What was that?

3   BETH: I think the front glass broke.

4   FRANKIE: It's getting bad out there!

5   BETH: As long as we don't hear a train …

6   FRANKIE: A train?

7   BETH: Tornadoes sound like trains.

8   FRANKIE: Are you scared?

9   BETH: I'm a little nervous.

10   FRANKIE: I'm more than a little nervous!

11   BETH: We'll be all right.

12   FRANKIE: Why don't they turn off those sirens?

13   BETH: I'm sure the National Weather Service saw something
14   on the radar.

15   FRANKIE: Beth, I'm really scared!

16   BETH: I know, Frankie. But it's going to be over soon. I know.
17   Why don't we make some plans?

18   FRANKIE: Plans?

19   BETH: Plans to have breakfast together in the morning? What
20   time do you get off work?

21   FRANKIE: Six a.m.

22   BETH: That's perfect. If you want to, that is.

23   FRANKIE: If the tornado doesn't kill us, sure.

24   BETH: And we'll talk about you singing at Eddie's.

25   FRANKIE: And you working at Channel Nine.

26   BETH: And maybe a few years from now, I'll be that
27   anchorperson who will be reporting about the new and
28   upcoming star from our very own hometown. Maybe
29   you'll grant me an interview?

30   FRANKIE: Of course I will. Did you hear that?

31   BETH: I did. Why don't we move back against the wall?

32   FRANKIE: *(As they step back)* Beth, I think I hear a train!

33   BETH: Maybe not.

34   FRANKIE: The lights! What happened to the lights?

35   BETH: It'll be OK, Frankie.

1   FRANKIE: I don't like this! I don't like this at all!

2   BETH: Let's sit down and cover our heads.

3   FRANKIE: It's coming, isn't it?

4   BETH: Come on. Let's sit down. *(They both sit down.)* And let's

5   put our hands over our heads. Like this. Come on.

6   FRANKIE: *(Covers her head.)* I really don't like this! I'm only

7   nineteen! I don't want to die!

8   BETH: We're not going to die. I know. Why don't you sing me

9   one of your songs?

10 FRANKIE: Now?

11 BETH: Sure.

12 FRANKIE: I will if you'll pretend you're outside in front of the

13   camera reporting on this storm!

14 BETH: All right. *(Clears throat.)* Folks, as you can see, it's very

15   windy out here tonight.

16 FRANKIE: I can hear the train, Beth!

17 BETH: Reports have been coming in that this storm produced

18   a large funnel cloud, but the good news is that it has

19   stayed to the edge of town and out in the open fields. The

20   worst damage seems to be uprooted trees, scattered

21   debris, and shattered windows from the golf-ball-size hail.

22   At this time, no injuries have been reported. The

23   meteorologist has just confirmed to me that we are out of

24   danger from this frightening storm. But we remind all

25   listeners to be careful as they get out and survey the

26   damage. Coming to you live, Beth Sanders from Channel

27   Nine News. *(Pause)* OK, your turn, Frankie. Let me hear

28   you sing.

29 FRANKIE: OK. The train may drown out my voice, but I'll sing.

30   *(Pauses, then sings.)* These country roads, lead me out of

31   here to the golden streets where dreams are found. These

32   country roads, take me away to find my dreams for

33   eternity.

34

35

16. Pablo

Cast: ISABEL and SHELLY
Setting: A bus stop

1   ISABEL: I hate waiting on the city bus.

2   SHELLY: Me too.

3   ISABEL: Sometimes they're on time, but most of the time —

4   SHELLY: They're late. My car is in the shop this week.

5   ISABEL: So you're stuck with the lovely city bus?

6   SHELLY: Yes. I'm on my way to work.

7   ISABEL: Where's that?

8   SHELLY: The Meridian Reporter.

9   ISABEL: You work at the newspaper?

10 SHELLY: Yes, that's right.

11 ISABEL: What do you do there?

12 SHELLY: I write.

13 ISABEL: Write anything exciting?

14 SHELLY: Let's see ... This week I wrote an article addressing the
15   school bus transportation problems. Can you imagine
16   where I got the idea for my story?

17 ISABEL: City bus to school bus?

18 SHELLY: Exactly. It reminded me of all the complaints we had
19   received in the opinion page, so I went with it. I could
20   especially relate to the tardiness issue. *(Glances at her
21   watch.)* Not your most exciting material, but we have space
22   to fill.

23 ISABEL: Sounds like you need a more interesting topic. Besides
24   waiting on the city bus.

25 SHELLY: Yes, more than you realize. Today I'm working on a
26   piece regarding the controversy of the city's plan to

1   upgrade the sewer lines.

2   ISABEL: Not to hurt your feelings, but I'd probably skip over
3   that story.

4   SHELLY: You and everyone else. Sometimes my own stories put
5   me to sleep.

6   ISABEL: So, what was the most exciting story you wrote?

7   SHELLY: Oh, that's easy to answer. There haven't been that
8   many, but one of the most interesting stories I covered
9   was on the armored car heist by those three former high
10   school football players. From Friday night heroes to
11   handcuffed teens who faced federal charges and prison
12   time.

13   ISABEL: That happened last year, right?

14   SHELLY: Two years ago. And since then it's been
15   transportation issues, sewer lines, local elections, the
16   grand opening of Daylight Donuts, and articles on our
17   local celebrities.

18   ISABEL: Here? We have local celebrities in this town?

19   SHELLY: Of course we do. There's Adeline Bishop, the oldest
20   woman in Baxter County. And there's Russ Mathews who
21   self-published his book, *The Untold Story of Russ*
22   *Matthews.* Mr. Hanson who received the Korean Service
23   Medal for his time spent in the Navy. Mrs. Milton who was
24   named President of the Quilting Club. Mr. Warner for fifty
25   years of service with Meridian County.

26   ISABEL: Did you enjoy writing those pieces?

27   SHELLY: Oh, they were somewhat interesting, but still not
28   exactly what I'd imagined writing about when I decided to
29   become a journalist.

30   ISABEL: But there must be an art to taking a dull story and
31   making it sound interesting.

32   SHELLY: Yes, that's true. And I do try to make the most of some
33   of my dullest stories. Like the one I wrote last week about
34   Ralph Tefferteller's struggles of growing up during the
35   Great Depression.

1 ISABEL: Sounds depressing.

2 SHELLY: And who wants to read about that? He's a grouchy old

3   man who has nothing kind to say. How do you write about

4   that?

5 ISABEL: Sounds difficult.

6 SHELLY: It was agonizing. And of course we have our famous

7   Randy Perkins who almost, just almost got to play for the

8   Dallas Cowboys.

9 ISABEL: What happened?

10 SHELLY: He got cut, but he came close. Very, very close. So close

11   it's been on the front page of our local Sunday section on

12   at least three occasions.

13 ISABEL: Wow. Local celebrities right here in this town.

14 SHELLY: That's right. And for the city of Meridian, Adeline

15   Bishop, Russ Matthews, and Randy Perkins are

16   considered local heroes who did something spectacular ...

17   or almost did something spectacular.

18 ISABEL: So it sounds like you're in the need of a good story.

19 SHELLY: In dire need of a good story. A story so amazing that it

20   would be picked up by other newspapers across the

21   country and send my career flying.

22 ISABEL: A story that you wouldn't dare skim over.

23 SHELLY: Exactly. But unfortunately for now, I'm stuck with the

24   upcoming school bond election. Yawn, right?

25 ISABEL: You know, I might have a story for you.

26 SHELLY: What? We have another local celebrity in our midst?

27   So tell me, what have you accomplished? Oh, let me grab

28   my notepad here. What is your name?

29 ISABEL: Isabel.

30 SHELLY: I'm Shelly.

31 ISABEL: Nice to meet you, Shelly.

32 SHELLY: All right, tell me about your accomplishments, Isabel.

33 ISABEL: Oh, it's not about me. I'm not a celebrity.

34 SHELLY: Someone in your family, then?

35 ISABEL: No. This is more like an undercover story you might be

1   interested in investigating.

2 SHELLY: Oh, now we're talking. Last undercover story I

3   covered was on the theft of carbonated beverages at the

4   courthouse. Apparently the girls in the District Clerk's

5   office found a Fonzie spot in the coke machine.

6 ISABEL: A Fonzie spot?

7 SHELLY: You know, like Fonzie from *Happy Days?* You hit

8   something in the right place and, well, anyway, the girls

9   could bang on the machine and cause it to dispense free

10   beverages.

11 ISABEL: You did undercover work on that?

12 SHELLY: I did. Sat near the pop machine for days wearing a wig

13   and sunglasses. The girls never even noticed I was there.

14   *(Leans over.)* Don't ever tell anyone this, but I actually gave

15   the machine a few of my own Fonzie hits — worked like

16   magic.

17 ISABEL: Well, this assignment would be a little more, well, a

18   little more emotional.

19 SHELLY: Perfect. It'll get my readers involved.

20 ISABEL: But you can't use my name.

21 SHELLY: That's not a problem. I always protect my sources. If

22   you choose to remain anonymous, then that's the way it'll

23   be.

24 ISABEL: You promise not to use my name?

25 SHELLY: *(Notices her seriousness.)* I promise, Isabel.

26 ISABEL: *(Looks around.)* Can we move over there to talk?

27 SHELLY: Sure.

28 ISABEL: I've told the police about what was going on, but they

29   didn't believe me.

30 SHELLY: And this isn't a joke?

31 ISABEL: No, I promise.

32 SHELLY: OK. Tell me what's going on.

33 ISABEL: It's my neighbor. He had this kid.

34 SHELLY: And?

35 ISABEL: And I don't think it's his kid. I'm not sure, but I don't

1   think it is.
2   SHELLY: Why not?
3   ISABEL: Because his skin is a different color.
4   SHELLY: So your neighbor has a kid living at his house that's a
5   different nationality? Isabel, he was probably adopted.
6   ISABEL: Forget it. I don't think you're going to believe me
7   either.
8   SHELLY: I'm listening, Isabel.
9   ISABEL: OK. Well, two weeks ago I went back to the police and
10   they said that if I came in with my outrageous lie again,
11   they were going to lock me up!
12 SHELLY: Really?
13 ISABEL: I don't exactly live in the best part of town. Actually,
14   it's the worst part of town. On the south side.
15 SHELLY: OK. Go on.
16 ISABEL: But it's the house next door to me.
17 SHELLY: Where your neighbor lives with his child?
18 ISABEL: Yes. And I've seen what he does to that little boy.
19 SHELLY: How old is he?
20 ISABEL: Seven. Eight. Maybe nine. I'm not exactly sure.
21 SHELLY: Does he go to school?
22 ISABEL: Oh no! He never leaves the house!
23 SHELLY: So how do you know all this?
24 ISABEL: Because late at night, my neighbor lets this boy go
25   outside in the backyard.
26 SHELLY: At night?
27 ISABEL: Yes. It's always late at night, like around midnight.
28 SHELLY: So he only lets him go outside at night to play?
29 ISABEL: He's not really going outside to play.
30 SHELLY: Then what's he doing?
31 ISABEL: I'm not sure, but he puts him on a chain. Like a dog.
32 SHELLY: Are you serious?
33 ISABEL: I swear.
34 SHELLY: And you've seen this?
35 ISABEL: Look, I'm not lying, even though no one believes me.

1   SHELLY: It just seems hard to believe.
2   ISABEL: I sit in my backyard a lot. I smoke, OK?
3   SHELLY: And you see your neighbor's son —
4   ISABEL: It's not his son.
5   SHELLY: And you see this boy chained up like a dog?
6   ISABEL: Yes. But only at night.
7   SHELLY: Have you ever tried to talk to this boy?
8   ISABEL: I have. We whisper through the fence. The first night I
9   whispered, "Hey, are you OK?"
10 SHELLY: What did he say?
11 ISABEL: Nothing.
12 SHELLY: Nothing. And you're sure this boy is chained up in the
13   backyard?
14 ISABEL: I knew you wouldn't believe me! Forget it!
15 SHELLY: No, no! I'm just trying to understand!
16 ISABEL: Well, for a long time he didn't talk. But one night I
17   threw a candy bar over the fence and he quickly ate it
18   before the neighbor came back outside. Then the next
19   night, I did it again. This time I put a little note with the
20   candy bar and told him to do something like sneeze if he
21   needed help.
22 SHELLY: And did he?
23 ISABEL: No.
24 SHELLY: He didn't? But you're still convinced something is
25   terribly wrong?
26 ISABEL: Yes. You don't believe me, do you?
27 SHELLY: I'm not sure. I want to, but … I don't know.
28 ISABEL: His name is Pablo.
29 SHELLY: He told you?
30 ISABEL: No, but I heard my neighbor screaming his name.
31   Every night, even if it's cold, I go outside and sit next to my
32   fence and whisper to Pablo.
33 SHELLY: And what do you say?
34 ISABEL: I say things like, "I'm here, Pablo. I'm going to help
35   you." Last week for the first time he responded.

1   SHELLY: What did he say?

2   ISABEL Help me.

3   SHELLY: How long has all this been going on?

4   ISABEL: About three months. I told you, I went to the police on

5   more than one occasion, but they didn't believe me. The

6   last time I went there, they threatened to arrest me.

7   Officer Landon threatened to tie me up by a chain outside

8   the station until I stopped coming in with lies.

9   SHELLY: Those idiots!

10   ISABEL: You believe me?

11   SHELLY: Knowing our local police officers, yes!

12   ISABEL: Every night I consider jumping the fence and

13   grabbing Pablo, but I've been afraid. What if my neighbor

14   has a gun and he shoots both of us?

15   SHELLY: Come on. Let's go.

16   ISABEL: Where are we going?

17   SHELLY: To CPS.

18   ISABEL: What's that?

19   SHELLY: Child Protective Services. Once we tell them your

20   story, they will call the authorities and have the house

21   surrounded in a matter of minutes. My friend Bethany

22   works at CPS. She'll believe us. And CPS checks out every

23   complaint.

24   ISABEL: Oh, Shelly, thank you! Thank you for believing me!

25   SHELLY: Yes, this could be a huge story, but more than that, I'm

26   concerned about this little boy. You know, it's possible he's

27   an abducted child.

28   ISABEL: I wondered about that, but when no one would believe

29   me ...

30   SHELLY: First, we need to get this kid rescued from what you

31   described as the pits of hell.

32   ISABEL: And then you can write your story.

33   SHELLY: Yes, but you know what, Isabel?

34   ISABEL: What?

35   SHELLY: I don't think you should remain anonymous. You

1   begging the authorities to listen to you and then trying to
2   find a plan to rescue him yourself, that says a lot about
3   you.
4   ISABEL: Oh no. I'm not a local celebrity. I just want to see Pablo
5   happy. I want to see him play outside in the sunlight with
6   the other children, not tied to a chain. You can have your
7   story. I just want Pablo free.
8   SHELLY: So do I. But you will ultimately be a very important
9   part of my story.
10 ISABEL: You help to free Pablo and you can use my name and
11   interview me all you want.
12 SHELLY: It's a good plan. Let's go!
13
14
15
16
17
18
19
20
21
22
23
24
25
26
27
28
29
30
31
32
33
34
35

17. Invisible

Cast: SHELBY and CHEYENNE
Setting: Back of the drama classroom

1   *(At rise, CHEYENNE is standing with her arms crossed,*
2   *staring at the floor. Her hair is in her face.)*
3   **SHELBY: What's wrong with you?**
4   **CHEYENNE: Why are you talking to me?**
5   **SHELBY: Excuse me?**
6   **CHEYENNE: Oh, I guess it's because no one else is around.**
7   **Right?**
8   **SHELBY: What are you talking about?**
9   **CHEYENNE: You never talk to me.**
10   **SHELBY: And you never talk to me. So I guess we're even.**
11   **Seriously, Cheyenne, what is your problem? Why do you**
12   **always exclude yourself from everyone?**
13   **CHEYENNE: Maybe I'm trying to avoid conflict.**
14   **SHELBY: Conflict?**
15   **CHEYENNE: Yes. Because the next person that I see roll their**
16   **eyes at me, I might just shove them into eternity.**
17   **SHELBY: That's nice. Another likeable feature about you. If you**
18   **can't join them, beat them up. That'll surely help you to**
19   **make friends.**
20   **CHEYENNE: Who said I want to make friends?**
21   **SHELBY: It's obvious that you don't.**
22   **CHEYENNE: And it's obvious you don't know a thing about me.**
23   **SHELBY: Well, tell me this, if you walked into a room and saw**
24   **yourself —**
25   **CHEYENNE: Wait! Is this reverse psychology? I walk in a room**
26   **and see me, but I'm not me, I'm someone else? And when**

1   I see me what do I think of me? The antisocial person in
2   the back corner with her head down?
3 SHELBY: Don't leave out unfriendly and angry.
4 CHEYENNE: Antisocial, unfriendly, and angry? *(Points.)* That
5   person over there? What do I think of her?
6 SHELBY: Yeah.
7 CHEYENNE: I think I'd want to stay away from that girl!
8 SHELBY: Exactly.
9 CHEYENNE: And I'd probably roll my eyes at her, too.
10 SHELBY: So why would you expect others to react any
11   differently?
12 CHEYENNE: You're right, Shelby. I'm an antisocial person who
13   can't handle social interaction. So, you know what? You
14   better hurry up and leave!
15 SHELBY: But don't you think it's odd?
16 CHEYENNE: Of course. Everyone thinks I'm odd. Heck, I think
17   I'm odd!
18 SHELBY: I mean that an introvert like yourself would sign up
19   for drama. Why put yourself through the agony?
20 CHEYENNE: You're right. What's wrong with me? How dare I
21   enroll in drama?
22 SHELBY: You come into class knowing you hate to socialize or
23   draw attention to yourself. Why?
24 CHEYENNE: You know, I should be examined by the country's
25   top psychologists to figure this one out.
26 SHELBY: And you sit in the back of the room, away from
27   everyone else. You refuse to participate. Refuse to talk.
28 CHEYENNE: Believe it or not, Shelby, I like the theatre class.
29 SHELBY: But ... ?
30 CHEYENNE: But I find it painful to interact in crowds.
31 SHELBY: Why?
32 CHEYENNE: I don't know. I don't even understand it myself.
33   Because when I'm alone, say in my room, I can see myself
34   as a sociable person. I'm talkative, happy, laughing. "Hey,
35   did you hear about this?" Or "Hey, did you hear about

1   that?" I can see it all so clearly. But when I step out of my
2   house and into a crowd, my mind shuts off and I find
3   myself wanting, no, *needing* to be alone. I don't blame
4   anyone for not wanting to be around me. Sure I'd rather
5   blame you, blame them, but ... it's me. It's all me.

6 SHELBY: I guess you're one of those loners.

7 CHEYENNE: Creepy and pathetic, right?

8 SHELBY: I didn't say that.

9 CHEYENNE: So now that we've diagnosed my personality ...

10 SHELBY: I was just trying to understand.

11 CHEYENNE: I'm an antisocial loner who is withdrawn and
12   angry at the world. Thanks, Shelby. Maybe I should
13   withdraw from society all together to spare everyone from
14   my psychological issues. You think?

15 SHELBY: I think you should try another approach.

16 CHEYENNE: Really? What's that?

17 SHELBY: You should force yourself to blend.

18 CHEYENNE: Blend?

19 SHELBY: Move to the front of the class. Hold your head up high.
20   And if you find it hard to talk to others, then at least smile.

21 CHEYENNE: Appear to be normal?

22 SHELBY: Yes. And maybe if you pretend that you have
23   confidence it will help you step out of your comfort zone.

24 CHEYENNE: Oh, so it's like I'm playing a part in a play.

25 SHELBY: Yes. As if you were on stage.

26 CHEYENNE: Then I become someone else.

27 SHELBY: If you want to look at it that way.

28 CHEYENNE: So I take on a role that gives me the ability to
29   comfortably socialize with others?

30 SHELBY: Exactly. And you push that hair out of your face, move
31   to the front of the room, and –

32 CHEYENNE: *(Looking around)* It's uncomfortable to stand up
33   there and not want to be invisible.

34 SHELBY: But you're playing a role. So you don't want to be
35   invisible, right?

1   **CHEYENNE: Right.**

2   **SHELBY: You want to be noticed. And as we've learned in the**

3   **drama class, you must take on your part and feel each and**

4   **every emotion.**

5   **CHEYENNE: But I'm not sure I know what part I have.**

6   **SHELBY: It's the Cheyenne you described when you're home**

7   **alone. The one who is happy, outgoing, and excited about**

8   **life.**

9   **CHEYENNE:** *(Smiles.)* **With no fears to hold me back. Who's also**

10   **a bit mysterious.**

11   **SHELBY: Mysterious? I like that.**

12   **CHEYENNE: And when I look across the room at him —**

13   **SHELBY: Him?**

14   **CHEYENNE: That boy in theatre class. Louis.**

15   **SHELBY: Louis, huh?**

16   **CHEYENNE: I give him one of my mysterious smiles and he**

17   **responds.** *(Pushes the hair from her face.)* **It's as if I control**

18   **my own destiny.**

19   **SHELBY: You do.**

20   **CHEYENNE: And the lines I've memorized —**

21   **SHELBY: In our play?**

22   **CHEYENNE: No, not that play, but in my life. The lines of my**

23   **life that I've rehearsed in my room when I'm all alone.**

24   **And it always flows so easily and naturally.**

25   **SHELBY: You're a star in your own play, Cheyenne.**

26   **CHEYENNE: Yes. Why haven't I thought of this before?**

27   **SHELBY: It doesn't matter. But what does matter is that you see**

28   **yourself in a new light now and that you become that**

29   **person.**

30   **CHEYENNE: But Shelby, that person doesn't really exist.**

31   **SHELBY: Of course she does. If it's you who creates her, then it**

32   **is you.**

33   **CHEYENNE: I guess ... Let me think about this.** *(Paces.)* **So I'm**

34   **not me, but her.**

35   **SHELBY: Don't think so hard about this. It's you.**

1   **CHEYENNE: No.**

2   **SHELBY: Who you want to become?**

3   **CHEYENNE: But when I look in the mirror ...**

4   **SHELBY: You see a person who you admire.**

5   **CHEYENNE: No.**

6   **SHELBY: The person who you become when you're all alone.**

7   **When there's no one around to cause you to have doubts**

8   **about yourself.**

9   **CHEYENNE: But it's not real.**

10   **SHELBY: It is real.**

11   **CHEYENNE: But the exhaustion.**

12   **SHELBY: What?**

13   **CHEYENNE: The exhaustion of interaction. The crowds. It**

14   **makes me want to withdraw. To become invisible.**

15   **SHELBY: No, Cheyenne. It's your new role now, remember?**

16   **CHEYENNE: I'm trying.**

17   **SHELBY: Close your eyes. Think of that person you want to**

18   **become.**

19   **CHEYENNE:** *(Closes eyes.)* **Yes, I want to be her.**

20   **SHELBY: Feel her emotions. Feel her confidence.**

21   **CHEYENNE: I'm happy. And I feel strong.**

22   **SHELBY: Look across the room at Louis. What is he doing?**

23   **CHEYENNE: He's smiling at me.**

24   **SHELBY: Are you smiling back?**

25   **CHEYENNE: Yes.**

26   **SHELBY: Go to him.**

27   **CHEYENNE: I can't.**

28   **SHELBY: Yes, you can. Walk over to him.**

29   **CHEYENNE: I ... I want to.**

30   **SHELBY: You can.**

31   **CHEYENNE:** *(Opens eyes.)* **I can't! I'm not ready.**

32   **SHELBY: OK, well that was a good start. Now think about our**

33   **theatre class and the play we are working on. Are you**

34   **going to try out for a part tomorrow? Wait. Don't answer.**

35   **CHEYENNE: No, I –**

1   SHELBY: What part would you want? If you could choose.

2   CHEYENNE: What part? Uh ... Dominique.

3   SHELBY: Good choice. Do you know the lines?

4   CHEYENNE: Yes.

5   SHELBY: Good. And I'll be her sister.

6   CHEYENNE: As if we're trying out for the parts?

7   SHELBY: Yes. Let's practice.

8   CHEYENNE: Well, all right. I guess.

9   SHELBY: OK, so I'm Grace, Dominique's sister. *(Short pause)*

10   Dominique, you should get rid of Tom.

11   CHEYENNE: I should, but I don't want to.

12   SHELBY: That man is not a good suitor for you.

13   CHEYENNE: Perhaps. But what do you know of men?

14   SHELBY: I know of Tom's reputation. Not to mention that his

15   social standing is not suitable for our family. Mother even

16   said so.

17   CHEYENNE: Mother only wishes for me to marry Philippe.

18   SHELBY: And a good provider he would be.

19   CHEYENNE: I am not looking for a provider.

20   SHELBY: Love?

21   CHEYENNE: Of course.

22   SHELBY: Don't let Mother hear you speak of loving Tom.

23   CHEYENNE: I never said that I loved him.

24   SHELBY: You won't admit it, but I know.

25   CHEYENNE: No, I won't admit it. Wait! Let me tell you

26   something! I will admit it! I will!

27   SHELBY: No, Dominique. It's dangerous to speak it out loud.

28   CHEYENNE: I don't care!

29   SHELBY: You don't care that our mother can't bear such talk?

30   Dominique, our mother wants you to marry someone who

31   is respectable!

32   CHEYENNE: What if I don't care about that?

33   SHELBY: You don't care about our mother?

34   CHEYENNE: I care about Tom! I love him, Grace! Do you hear

35   me? I love him!

1   SHELBY: Stop it! Don't say that out loud! You know if she hears
2   you she will send you away.
3   CHEYENNE: To Winchester.
4   SHELBY: Yes. So she can stop you from running off with Tom.
5   CHEYENNE: I did not say I was running off with Tom. And
6   sending me to Aunt Vivian's will not change how I feel.
7   SHELBY: It's not about how you feel.
8   CHEYENNE: Not about how I feel? Of course it is! We've been
9   saving money. And we may just run away. And I don't care!
10   I don't care what you or Mother says. And if you tell her ...
11 SHELBY: I won't, Dominique! Of course I won't!
12 CHEYENNE: But if you do, I will never speak to you again. Ever.
13   And I will not be sent away to Winchester! I will not be told
14   whom I can or can't love!
15 SHELBY: Even if it's for your own good?
16 CHEYENNE: It's not for my own good if I'm not happy!
17 SHELBY: I don't know, Dominique.
18 CHEYENNE: Then we shall see what happens.
19 SHELBY: Yes, we shall see. *(Pause)* That was good, Cheyenne.
20 CHEYENNE: I like that part. I can imagine fighting for Louis
21   like that.
22 SHELBY: You surprised me. You're a good actress.
23 CHEYENNE: Really?
24 SHELBY: Really.
25 CHEYENNE: Thank you.
26 SHELBY: And you should definitely audition for the part of
27   Dominique.
28 CHEYENNE: But the competition ... Arianna, Bridget ... you ...
29   There's no way I'd get the part.
30 SHELBY: Cheyenne, you have just as good a chance as anyone
31   else.
32 CHEYENNE: You really think so?
33 SHELBY: Yes! OK, picture yourself at auditions tomorrow.
34   Script in hand, you and I on stage. I'll read with you just
35   like we did today.

1 CHEYENNE: With everyone staring?

2 SHELBY: It'll be just the two of us on stage.

3 CHEYENNE: Arianna hates me. She'll be staring at me.

4 SHELBY: That doesn't matter.

5 CHEYENNE: *(Head down)* I don't know.

6 SHELBY: Just like today. I'll read the part of Grace and you'll

7   read the part of Dominique.

8 CHEYENNE: I don't know.

9 SHELBY: You're a good actress, Cheyenne.

10 CHEYENNE: You know, suddenly I feel as if I can't breathe.

11 SHELBY: You can breathe. It's just you and me and —

12 CHEYENNE: *(Breathless)* No, I need ... I need to step back ... I ...

13 SHELBY: What are you afraid of?

14 CHEYENNE: I don't know ... I ...

15 SHELBY: You're that actress in your bedroom. The actress with

16   confidence. Who smiles across the room at Louis. Who

17   gives him that mysterious smile. And he smiles back,

18   remember? You're beautiful, talented —

19 CHEYENNE: I ... I'm trying ...

20 SHELBY: And the auditions have begun. We're on the stage.

21   You're Dominique and I'm your sister Grace. And I say,

22   "You should get rid of Tom." Then you say ...

23 CHEYENNE: I ... I ... I ... *(Looking around)* They're all staring at me!

24   Arianna is laughing! Louis is rolling his eyes! I want to run

25   off the stage as fast as I can!

26 SHELBY: No, no! You can do this.

27 CHEYENNE: No! What I want is to be invisible!

28 SHELBY: Cheyenne, come on!

29 CHEYENNE: No, I can't! I can't do this! You don't know how

30   hard this is for me! Yes, I want to pretend that I'm that

31   confident person who looks around the room and

32   interacts with people. Who throws a mysterious glance at

33   Louis and he responds. Who ignores the laughs from

34   Arianna and Bridget. Who auditions for the part of

35   Dominique and actually lands it. But I'm dealing with me!

1   *Me!* And I know for a fact that I'm none of those things!
2   SHELBY: Cheyenne, you can become whoever you want.
3   CHEYENNE: Good. Because I want to be invisible.
4
5
6
7
8
9
10
11
12
13
14
15
16
17
18
19
20
21
22
23
24
25
26
27
28
29
30
31
32
33
34
35

18. The Red Dress

Cast: KIMBER and JACI
Setting: Student Center at a junior college

1   KIMBER: What was all of that about?

2   JACI: What?

3   KIMBER: You and Bryan.

4   JACI: We were just talking.

5   KIMBER: It looked like more than that to me.

6   JACI: Bryan and I have a couple of classes together. Sometimes
7   we study together. Well, mostly he tutors me. Chemistry is
8   killing me.

9   KIMBER: Oh! For a minute there it looked like you were
10   flirting with him. But you wouldn't do that. Not with *him*.

11 JACI: Why do you say that?

12 KIMBER: What do you mean, *Why do I say that?* Look at him!

13 JACI: *(Looks toward BRYAN.)* I think he's pretty amazing.

14 KIMBER: Are you serious?

15 JACI: Yes.

16 KIMBER: Whoa! Hold on a minute. You mean as a friend, right?

17 JACI: Yes, but —

18 KIMBER: But you'd never date him, right?

19 JACI: I didn't say that.

20 KIMBER: Of course you wouldn't! Who would? So, let me get
21   this straight. You're flirting with Bryan because he's a
22   whiz in chemistry and you need his help. Right?

23 JACI: I need his help, but it's not like that.

24 KIMBER: Then what are you doing?

25 JACI: Gosh, Kimber, you make it sound like I'm using him! I'm
26   not doing that!

1   KIMBER: Don't get so defensive, Jaci. I get it. So the two of you
2   are friends. OK. I'm sorry I jumped to the wrong
3   conclusion earlier.
4   JACI: Maybe you didn't.
5   KIMBER: What?
6   JACI: Let me ask you something, Kimber. If Eric was like Bryan,
7   would you still care about him?
8   KIMBER: *(Looks toward BRYAN.)* If Eric was like him? I don't
9   know. Probably not. I mean, I'd like him as a friend, but to
10   date Eric if he were like that? No. I couldn't do it.
11   JACI: I could.
12   KIMBER: What are you trying to tell me?
13   JACI: I'm trying to tell you that I like Bryan.
14   KIMBER: For more than a friend?
15   JACI: Yes.
16   KIMBER: Jaci! Come on! How could you be attracted to
17   someone like Bryan?
18   JACI: *(Looks toward BRYAN. After a pause)* Because I can see past
19   his wheelchair.
20   KIMBER: You're kidding, right?
21   JACI: Kimber, he's just like everyone else.
22   KIMBER: No, he's not!
23   JACI: Yes, he is!
24   KIMBER: OK, I'm not trying to be rude here, but you have
25   obviously lost your mind! Jaci, come on! You can't be that
26   desperate!
27   JACI: I'm not desperate! You know, forget it! I knew you
28   wouldn't understand!
29   KIMBER: Jaci, the guy's in a wheelchair!
30   JACI: I know that, Kimber!
31   KIMBER: And what could you possibly see in a guy like him?
32   JACI: For one thing, we have a lot in common.
33   KIMBER: Oh, sure.
34   JACI: And he makes me laugh. *(Smiles.)* Yesterday we went into
35   this costume shop and I don't remember when I've ever

1   laughed so hard. I tried on this long blonde wig and Bryan
2   said I looked like a princess. He found a tiara for me to
3   wear. He called me Princess Jaci as we walked through the
4   store. He even asked the salesclerk to bow to me as we
5   passed by. *(Laughs.)* And she did. And then Bryan found
6   these Elton John glasses and put them on. You know those
7   big silver frames in the shape of stars?
8   **KIMBER:** Elton John?
9   **JACI:** *(Nods as she laughs.)* And then he picked up this fake
10   microphone and started singing. In the store! Everyone
11   was looking! *(Imitates.)* ***And I guess that's why they call it***
12   ***the blues.*** *(Laughs.)* Well, not exactly like that. I can't sing.
13   But he can and he was great! And all the people around us
14   applauded and, well, it was great!
15   **KIMBER:** Bryan imitating Elton John?
16   **JACI:** And honestly, he has a great singing voice!
17   **KIMBER:** Jaci, what are you doing?
18   **JACI:** I'm trying to explain to you that Bryan is just a normal
19   guy.
20   **KIMBER:** No, he's not. Look at him! *(Pause as they look his*
21   *direction)* Jaci, I get it that you think Bryan is nice, smart,
22   has a good singing voice, and I suppose if you looked past
23   the wheelchair you could say he's cute —
24   **JACI:** I have no problem looking past his wheelchair, Kimber.
25   **KIMBER:** And with you and Matt calling it quits a few weeks
26   ago, it does make sense.
27   **JACI:** Kimber, this doesn't have anything to do with Matt and
28   me breaking up!
29   **KIMBER:** Of course it does! Think about it. You and Matt were
30   inseparable. Then he takes off to Texas State while you
31   stay here at the local junior college. I'm sure you're feeling
32   lonely.
33   **JACI:** I'm not lonely, Kimber! I'm glad Matt and I went our
34   separate ways. It was time.
35   **KIMBER:** Wow. You've sure changed your tune about that.

1　JACI: I have and it's a good thing. You know Matt hated the
2　　　　hours I spent at the gym. All he did was complain about
3　　　　how it took away from our time together. And now that
4　　　　I'm a part of the gymnastics team, I need to practice more
5　　　　than ever!
6　KIMBER: Does Bryan know you're a gymnast?
7　JACI: Yes. That's where I first saw him. He was in the gym
8　　　　watching us practice.
9　KIMBER: That seems odd. You wouldn't think a guy in a
10　　　　wheelchair would be interested in gymnastics.
11　JACI: Like I said, Kimber, you don't know anything about him.
12　KIMBER: I never said I did.
13　JACI: Bryan was a gymnast, too. He was injured while
14　　　　performing a floor routine his freshman year in high
15　　　　school.
16　KIMBER: He was a gymnast?
17　JACI: Yes.
18　KIMBER: What happened? I mean, what went wrong?
19　JACI: He was practicing his final tumbling pass and decided to
20　　　　add a triple twist to his routine. Something went wrong
21　　　　and he landed on his neck. He should've had a spotter, but
22　　　　he didn't. It was a bad decision with unexpected
23　　　　consequences.
24　KIMBER: How sad!
25　JACI: That's what caused him to be paralyzed from the waist
26　　　　down.
27　KIMBER: I didn't know.
28　JACI: Neither did I. I kept seeing him at our meets and
29　　　　wondered what he was doing there. I figured he was
30　　　　someone's brother or something. Then one day as I
31　　　　rounded the corner on my way to the Student Center I
32　　　　practically fell in his lap.
33　KIMBER: I bet that was embarrassing.
34　JACI: It was for about a second. Until he smiled at me.
35　KIMBER: He does have a nice smile.

1　JACI: And you should have seen me! I was a mess full of
2　　　apologies. But he just smiled and spoke to me in a calming
3　　　voice. Then right away we started talking about the last
4　　　gymnastics meet I'd had. He complimented me on my
5　　　balance beam performance and said he understood the
6　　　difficult moves I'd worked into my routine. And then the
7　　　small talk turned into lunch. And one lunch turned into
8　　　another. And before I knew it he was rescuing me from
9　　　having a chemistry meltdown. And now —
10　KIMBER: Now?
11　JACI: Now I can't imagine him not being a part of my life. He's
12　　　my best friend.
13　KIMBER: Jaci, I understand him being your friend, but more
14　　　than that ... ? *(Shakes her head.)*
15　JACI: And he's my biggest fan. When I go to a gymnastics meet,
16　　　his presence means everything to me. Somehow he calms
17　　　my fears. And on those occasions when the gym goes
18　　　silent and I hear those gasps from the spectators as I
19　　　wobble to catch my balance and stay on the beam, I feel
20　　　his support holding me up. And it does. He does. He gives
21　　　me a lot of strength, Kimber.
22　KIMBER: Jaci, how long has this been going on? Why didn't you
23　　　tell me?
24　JACI: I wanted to.
25　KIMBER: But you thought I wouldn't understand?
26　JACI: You didn't.
27　KIMBER: Jaci, I'm not trying to be negative here, but think
28　　　about it. Who dates a guy in a wheelchair? Seriously, you
29　　　don't want to do this!
30　JACI: Why not?
31　KIMBER: People are going to make fun of you.
32　JACI: I don't care.
33　KIMBER: Jaci, please! Stop and think about this!
34　JACI: I am! I have been!
35　KIMBER: You've thought about how your life would be if you

1   dated a guy confined to a wheelchair?

2   JACI: Yes!

3   KIMBER: So tell me this: Are you going to the Christmas dance

4   on the fifteenth?

5   JACI: I ... I don't know. I haven't really thought about that.

6   KIMBER: You were a few weeks ago! Remember? You were all

7   excited about borrowing my red dress and wearing it to

8   the dance.

9   JACI: I know ...

10   KIMBER: Think about it, Jaci! Eric and I will be out there

11   dancing and if you go with Bryan, what will you be doing?

12   Standing beside his wheelchair staring at everyone else

13   on the dance floor? The whole time wishing you were out

14   there twirling around in that red dress?

15   JACI: I don't know, Kimber! Bryan hasn't asked me to the dance

16   yet.

17   KIMBER: Good! Then find someone to go with besides a guy in

18   a wheelchair! Or go alone! It's going to be a blast, you

19   know. And afterwards, we can all go over to Eric's

20   apartment and hang out. Maybe stay up all night as we

21   celebrate the Christmas break. What do you say?

22   JACI: *(Looking off)* I ... I don't know.

23   KIMBER: And if Eric proposes during the holidays —

24   JACI: You think Eric's going to propose?

25   KIMBER: I'm almost sure of it. He's been asking me for my ring

26   size.

27   JACI: But what about school?

28   KIMBER: We can have a long engagement.

29   JACI: And you're sure about this? I mean, about Eric?

30   KIMBER: Of course I am! We're a perfect fit. His ability to play

31   any musical instrument, my desire to teach music ... we're

32   perfect together!

33   JACI: But I thought you were having second thoughts about

34   Eric.

35   KIMBER: Oh, you can't pay any attention to me.

1   JACI: But just last week you were crying because he was
2   criticizing you again.
3   KIMBER: Eric is a perfectionist. It beats the alternative, don't
4   you think?
5   JACI: But Kimber, Eric is always hurting your feelings.
6   KIMBER: So I need to toughen up, don't I? Besides, Eric has a
7   better understanding on how I should teach piano to my
8   first graders.
9   JACI: What makes him the expert?
10   KIMBER: He plays the piano better than I do.
11   JACI: So? You're teaching six-year-olds, Kimber!
12   KIMBER: I know. And at first I thought he was interfering, but
13   now I see that he's just offering some advice, which I'd
14   have to admit has been helpful.
15   JACI: And what about him insisting that you spend more hours
16   playing? Never mind the fact that you teach piano six days
17   a week. And have classes. And rehearsals.
18   KIMBER: Eric knows I'm not as dedicated as I should be. So he
19   pushes me. In a loving way, of course. And he pushes me
20   in other areas, too. What I eat. How I manage my time.
21   When I don't get enough sleep ... or sleep too much. He's
22   just wants the best for me.
23   JACI: And you can deal with that?
24   KIMBER: Of course! Eric's helping me work through my issues.
25   JACI: Your issues?
26   KIMBER: My problems with procrastination. Laziness.
27   Organization failures.
28   JACI: Really? Don't you think he should be more supportive
29   instead of critical?
30   KIMBER: He is supportive!
31   JACI: Kimber, do you realize Eric will always have that
32   controlling personality you constantly complain about?
33   KIMBER: Well then, it sounds like one of us needs to change,
34   doesn't it?
35   JACI: And you know it won't be him.

1 KIMBER: Jaci, why are you doing this? Why are you trying to
2   upset me when I just told you I think Eric is going to
3   propose during the holidays?
4 JACI: Because I want you to be happy, Kimber.
5 KIMBER: Which I am. Which is what I want for you, too. Which
6   is why I told you to dump the wheelchair guy and find
7   someone who can fling you around the dance floor in
8   your red dress. That is, *my* red dress.
9 JACI: I do want to go to the dance.
10 KIMBER: Then that's what you'll do! We'll all go together. You,
11   me, Eric ...
12 JACI: But I want to go with Bryan.
13 KIMBER: And do what? Sit there?
14 JACI: Truthfully, Kimber, I'd rather sit there and talk to Bryan
15   than be with someone I don't care about.
16 KIMBER: Really?
17 JACI: Yes. We can talk, laugh, enjoy the music —
18 KIMBER: But you shouldn't settle for less, Jaci! And besides,
19   Eric would absolutely refuse to hang around a guy like
20   Bryan.
21 JACI: And so would you, right?
22 KIMBER: Jaci, how can the four of us have fun if he's your date?
23 JACI: It wouldn't be that difficult, Kimber!
24 KIMBER: I don't understand you! How could you even consider
25   going with Bryan to the dance? You're an incredible
26   dancer! And you wearing that red dress ... all wasted! And
27   for what? Good conversation?
28 JACI: Yes! Good conversation filled with laughter, seriousness,
29   silliness, or whatever else we feel like doing!
30 KIMBER: I'm telling you, Jaci, Eric won't let us hang around
31   you if you bring Bryan.
32 JACI: That's fine, Kimber, because I won't let Bryan hang
33   around Eric! How about that?
34 KIMBER: How could you say that?
35 JACI: In fact, tonight I'm going to ask Bryan to go with me to the

1   dance. *(Smiles.)* I'm sure he'll say yes. And never mind
2   about me borrowing your red dress! I'll get my own!
3   KIMBER: Why are you doing this?
4   JACI: I have to go.
5   KIMBER: Where are you going?
6   JACI: To find a red dress.
7   KIMBER: Jaci! Why?
8   JACI: Because I don't see his wheelchair, Kimber. I see him. And
9   when we go to that dance together, I want him to see me
10   for who I am.
11 KIMBER: And who is that?
12 JACI: Someone without disappointments or regrets. Someone
13   without the fear of narrow-minded people. Someone who
14   sees him for who he is. And all of that wrapped up into a
15   red dress. And it will be a wonderful night!
16
17
18
19
20
21
22
23
24
25
26
27
28
29
30
31
32
33
34
35

19. Inner Pain

Cast: JADE and AMBER
Setting: School

1   *(At rise, AMBER is interviewing JADE for a paper she is going*
2   *to write.)*
3   JADE: I'd hardly say we're friends.
4   AMBER: What does that mean?
5   JADE: We're hardly friends.
6   AMBER: Hardly?
7   JADE: We're not.
8   AMBER: Then would you say we're enemies?
9   JADE: Enemies? No.
10   AMBER: Strangers?
11   JADE: No. I've known you since the seventh grade.
12   AMBER: But what do you know about me?
13   JADE: Well, I know your name is Amber. I know you don't
14   usually talk very much, which surprised me when you
15   wanted to interview me for your assignment. And let's see,
16   what else? Oh, you like to read. You read a lot. You've
17   always got your nose stuck in a book. And, well, I guess
18   that's it.
19   AMBER: That's it?
20   JADE: Pretty much.
21   AMBER: If that's all, then you don't really know me. Not really.
22   JADE: What's there to know?
23   AMBER: Hold on a minute. I'm asking the questions here.
24   JADE: Fine. But before I answer any more of your questions, I'd
25   like to know what the topic is of your assignment.
26   AMBER: Well, I'm trying to show that two people, like you and

1   me, can become friends even though we're miles apart on

2   the popularity meter.

3 JADE: I don't have to agree with your theory, do I?

4 AMBER: No, but when this is over, I think you'll agree.

5 JADE: Agree that we can be friends? You and me?

6 AMBER: Yes.

7 JADE: Wait a minute. Is this assignment really a cover for

8   something else?

9 AMBER: Like what?

10 JADE: Like your way of trying to move into my world? Hoping

11   you can hang out with me and springboard off of my

12   popularity?

13 AMBER: No!

14 JADE: Because that would never happen.

15 AMBER: Jade, this is not an effort to become popular! That's

16   not the issue!

17 JADE: Then what is the issue?

18 AMBER: It's two people, you and me, who appear to have

19   absolutely nothing in common —

20 JADE: We don't.

21 AMBER: You're way up there on the popularity meter —

22 JADE: And you're the definition of antisocial. Except for today.

23   You've surprised me.

24 AMBER: Who shops in the finest stores. A fashion expert it

25   would seem.

26 JADE: While you ...

27 AMBER: I like to dress comfortably.

28 JADE: I was going to say dull and drab, but I didn't want to hurt

29   your feelings.

30 AMBER: A cheerleader.

31 JADE: A spectator.

32 AMBER: A vote-for-me attitude.

33 JADE: Stare-at-your-feet attitude.

34 AMBER: Positive and happy.

35 JADE: Quiet and sad.

1   AMBER: Look at me!

2   JADE: Don't look at me.

3   AMBER: So, do you think we described each other accurately?

4   JADE: Pretty much. And the point is?

5   AMBER: The point is that despite all that, we share a secret.

6   Some would consider is quite disturbing.

7   JADE: A secret? You and me?

8   AMBER: Yes.

9   JADE: I don't think so!

10   AMBER: It will be clear to you very soon.

11   JADE: Look, Amber, you and me, we're nothing alike! Radically

12   different in every way possible. You could say we live on

13   two different planets. If two people could clash, that's you

14   and me!

15   AMBER: I have another question for you.

16   JADE: What?

17   AMBER: Tell me about the worst day of your life.

18   JADE: Wouldn't you rather hear about the best day of my life?

19   AMBER: No. Tell me what kills you on the inside. What eats at

20   you? What makes you want to scream?

21   JADE: Are you serious?

22   AMBER: Yes. I want to know.

23   JADE: Uh, look, I don't need the grade, Amber. So if that's it

24   with the questions, I'm out of here.

25   AMBER: Wait!

26   JADE: *(Annoyed)* What?

27   AMBER: Maybe I approached it all wrong. Maybe I should have

28   been more direct.

29   JADE: "Tell me about the worst day of your life" wasn't direct

30   enough?

31   AMBER: What I was trying to say was that we both —

32   JADE: What?

33   AMBER: That you and I ... we both ...

34   JADE: What?! Tell me?!

35   AMBER: *(Short pause)* We both cut ourselves.

1   JADE: What?

2   AMBER: I've seen your scars. I have them, too.

3   JADE: Look, I don't know what you're talking about!

4   AMBER: In gym class, when you pulled off your socks, I saw
5   them.

6   JADE: You saw what?

7   AMBER: Your scars.

8   JADE: You mean you saw where I cut myself shaving?

9   AMBER: I try to hide it, too. Especially from my mom.

10 JADE: Is this interview over with? Because I have things to do!

11 AMBER: I've been researching it on the Internet.

12 JADE: And you're going to write a paper about people cutting
13   themselves?

14 AMBER: Maybe.

15 JADE: Well, don't use my name in your stupid paper!

16 AMBER: You can remain anonymous.

17 JADE: Remain anonymous? I don't even want to be mentioned!

18 AMBER: Do you want to know what I learned about people who
19   cut?

20 JADE: No!

21 AMBER: I read that self-injury is caused from inner pain.

22 JADE: *(Uncomfortable laugh)* Inner pain? What's that?

23 AMBER: Could be anything. A way to cope with problems that
24   seem too difficult to bear. A bad situation you can't
25   change. Intense pressure. An upsetting relationship.
26   Rejection. Sorrow. Rage. Desperation. Emptiness.

27 JADE: Well, aren't you the expert! A walking expert right here!
28   Well, obviously this is your problem and not mine!

29 AMBER: But Jade, you're the only person I know who might
30   understand.

31 JADE: Well, maybe you better keep looking because I don't
32   understand!

33 AMBER: I'm not going to tell anyone if that's what you're
34   worried about.

35 JADE: You better not! Because it would be a big fat lie!

1   AMBER: You know, I hate doing it. I hate cutting myself.

2   JADE: Then stop!

3   AMBER: I can't! You know that!

4   JADE: Look, I'm not your counselor here!

5   AMBER: But this anger boils up inside of me to the point I feel
6   like I'm going to explode.

7   JADE: Like you want to scream?

8   AMBER: Yeah!

9   JADE: Or cry?

10 AMBER: Yeah! But I can't. I don't remember the last time I
11   cried.

12 JADE: You don't?

13 AMBER: No.

14 JADE: *(Pause)* Me neither.

15 AMBER: For some reason, the tears won't come. So, the only
16   way to deal with the pain, even if it's only temporary —

17 JADE: Is to cut.

18 AMBER: Yeah. Then I'm back in control of my life. And the way
19   I feel after I cut ...

20 JADE: Relieved.

21 AMBER: Like I can finally breathe.

22 JADE: I'm alive.

23 AMBER: And it's weird because I don't even feel any pain when
24   I take that knife and cut myself.

25 JADE: I use a razor blade. And I'm happy to see the blood. *(Short*
26   *pause)* Does your family know?

27 AMBER: No. Yours?

28 JADE: No! My mother wouldn't understand. She'd just whisk
29   me off to some wacko psychiatrist!

30 AMBER: My mother would cry. I don't want to see that.

31 JADE: I wouldn't either.

32 AMBER: Do you remember the first time you cut yourself?

33 JADE: Yes. It was the usual misery going on at home. My
34   stepdad ... his drinking, throwing things, screaming,
35   blaming. He was drunk one night and the remote control

1   broke. I think it needed new batteries. Well, anyway, he

2   got so mad. I mean, so mad! He took that remote control

3   and threw it across the room at me.

4 AMBER: Where was your mom?

5 JADE: I don't know. Out. Scrapbooking with her friends, I

6   think.

7 AMBER: What did you do?

8 JADE: What my stepdad told me to do. I picked up the remote

9   control and took it back to him. Of course it still didn't

10   work. I suggested new batteries, but he said it wasn't the

11   batteries. Then he blamed *me* for breaking it.

12 AMBER: You?

13 JADE: Apparently it was my fault. Then after slamming it into

14   my back as I walked away, he told me I couldn't watch TV

15   again.

16 AMBER: Wow.

17 JADE: I thought about running away, but where would I go?

18   Instead, I went to my room, opened up the drawer near

19   my desk, took out a pair of scissors, and cut myself.

20 AMBER: I'm sorry.

21 JADE: So what about you? How did it start for you?

22 AMBER: I don't remember the exact day, but it was last fall. I

23   came home from school after another horrible day. Riley

24   had shoved me in the hall for the hundredth time.

25 JADE: Why?

26 AMBER: Because I exist.

27 JADE: I'm sorry.

28 AMBER: And the day had gone as usual. No one to eat with at

29   lunch. Mr. Darcy getting mad at me in band. Other girls

30   ignoring me. Laughing. Teasing. Glares. When I got home

31   from school, I went to the kitchen for a snack but ended

32   up picking up a knife instead. I never told anyone before.

33 JADE: Me neither.

34 AMBER: And when I cut myself, I suddenly felt better.

35 JADE: Me too.

1   AMBER: But that feeling never lasts.
2   JADE: I know. Sometimes it only lasts for a few hours.
3   AMBER: Hopefully a day.
4   JADE: But then it happens again.
5   AMBER: And again.
6   JADE: Where do you cut?
7   AMBER: Mostly on my arms. That's why I'm always wearing
8   long-sleeved shirts.
9   JADE: You saw my ankles. I don't know what I'm going to do
10   when flip flop season arrives. Guess I'll wear tennis shoes
11   all summer.
12 AMBER: Some people cut themselves all over. Or use a cigarette
13   or match to burn their skin.
14 JADE: So there are a lot of us?
15 AMBER: I think so.
16 JADE: So in all this research you're doing, does it tell you how
17   to stop?
18 AMBER: Minus going to a counselor?
19 JADE: I'm not going to a counselor!
20 AMBER: Well, I read that we're supposed to express our
21   feelings instead of repressing them.
22 JADE: Easier said than done.
23 AMBER: We have to talk about it.
24 JADE: To who? My stepdad?! Maybe he could throw a few more
25   things at me! I'm sure that'll knock me into my senses!
26   And if I tried to talk to my mom, well, she wouldn't
27   understand. Or care. She's too busy with her little social
28   gatherings to listen to me. The High Society Women's
29   Club, a book club, volunteering at the hospital and the
30   food bank, gardening, scrapbooking ...
31 AMBER: I thought about talking to the school counselor.
32 JADE: You can't do that! Mrs. Billingsley would call your mom
33   in a heartbeat!
34 AMBER: I know. And my mom would just start crying. I can
35   hear her now. "Why are you trying to kill yourself?"

1   JADE: We're not trying to kill ourselves!

2   AMBER: No. I don't want to die. I just want the pain to stop.

3   JADE: Me too. OK, so we're supposed to talk about our feelings,

4   right?

5   AMBER: It's supposed to offer a great sense of relief. Talking to

6   someone you can trust.

7   JADE: Are you really writing a paper about cutting?

8   AMBER: No. I just wanted to find a way to talk to you about this.

9   JADE: I'm glad you did.

10   AMBER: And I thought maybe we could help each other.

11   JADE: It'd be nice to have someone to talk to.

12   AMBER: And I read that if some things are too difficult to

13   express, you should write it down.

14   JADE: I would read it and not judge you.

15   AMBER: Same here.

16   JADE: And we could call each other. You know, at those

17   moments. Maybe talk each other out of it.

18   AMBER: That might help.

19   JADE: And of course it'll be our secret.

20   AMBER: Yeah. No one else can ever find out.

21   JADE: No. Never. You want to have lunch with me today?

22   AMBER: What about your friends? What will they think?

23   JADE: I don't care about that. It's nice having someone to talk

24   to. Someone who really understands.

25   AMBER: I do.

26   JADE: And you're right.

27   AMBER: About what?

28   JADE: We are alike.

29

30

31

32

33

34

35

20. Broken Promises

Cast: ANNIE and TORI
Setting: Anywhere two girls can talk i.e., bedroom,
coffee shop, school cafeteria, etc.

1 ANNIE: Did I tell you he's getting married next week?

2 TORI: So soon?

3 ANNIE: Apparently they can't wait. As my father put it, "This
4   kind of love only comes around once in a lifetime."

5 TORI: Doesn't he mean twice in a lifetime?

6 ANNIE: Oh no! Dad has come to the realization that he never
7   loved my mother. So you know that old saying, "you were
8   conceived out of love"? Well, what am I supposed to think
9   now?

10 TORI: I think you should ignore him. Your father doesn't know
11   what he's saying.

12 ANNIE: Of course he knows what he's saying.

13 TORI: Annie, your father is still in the infatuation stage. He's
14   overloaded with endorphins and isn't thinking clearly.
15   Give him a few months to come back to reality.

16 ANNIE: Honestly, Tori, I don't care. Besides, by the time he
17   comes back to reality, he'll be hitched to Lacy.

18 TORI: How long has he been seeing her?

19 ANNIE: Since the day his divorce was final. A few months.

20 TORI: Wow. That's quick.

21 ANNIE: Tell me about it.

22 TORI: Are you going to the wedding?

23 ANNIE: No. Absolutely not.

24 TORI: Were you invited?

25 ANNIE: Oh yes. I'm supposed to meet the happy couple at the

1   courthouse on Friday to witness their lovely marriage by

2   the Justice of the Peace.

3   TORI: And it's a definite no?

4   ANNIE: Tori, there's no way I'd go! Seeing my dad with her. Oh!

5   TORI: Annie, it'll get easier with time.

6   ANNIE: You think I should be mature about it, don't you?

7   TORI: I think it's never easy for a child to see their parents

8   divorce. Even at our age. But then to get married again so

9   quickly ... I understand it's difficult.

10 ANNIE: How old were you when your parents divorced?

11 TORI: Seven.

12 ANNIE: Who left who?

13 TORI: I was told it was a mutual decision.

14 ANNIE: Because they fell out of love?

15 TORI: My parents never told me the reason they divorced, but

16   I guess it's because they fell out of love. Over the years it

17   was obvious they couldn't stand each other. Mom talked

18   bad about Dad. Dad talked bad about Mom. "Why won't

19   your mother ever give me a report card? Doesn't she

20   realize that I'm interested in your grades, too?" And Mom,

21   "Do you see that I have to do everything for you, Tori? Your

22   father can't even find the time to attend your dance

23   recitals or participate in the fundraisers you have at

24   school. Your dad only shows up when it doesn't interfere

25   with his own precious schedule." *(Short pause)* Yeah, I had

26   to listen to my parents bad mouth each other all the time.

27   I hated it.

28 ANNIE: I'm hearing that stuff from my mom now. I guess she

29   likes using me as her sounding board.

30 TORI: What does she say?

31 ANNIE: She says things like, "Your father is making a fool out

32   of himself, you know that, don't you? Getting involved

33   with someone half his age. What is he thinking? Does he

34   actually think he can carry on an intelligent conversation

35   with her? Well, of course he can't! And somehow he's

1 fooled her into thinking he's some wonderful flawless
2 human being. Well, she's got a rude awakening in front of
3 her! And you know it won't last. You and I both know why
4 he's with her."
5 TORI: That's got to be a pain to listen to.
6 ANNIE: Tori, how is it that two people can fall in love, get
7 married, have kids, and then wake up one day hating each
8 other?
9 TORI: I don't know, Annie.
10 ANNIE: I don't even know who my father is anymore.
11 TORI: I hardly see my father anymore. Except for the holidays.
12 ANNIE: Why is that?
13 TORI: Because he has another family now. He and Jill had
14 three kids. Two boys and a girl.
15 ANNIE: I didn't know you had siblings.
16 TORI: I don't talk about them much because we're not that
17 close. Maybe it's me. Because maybe deep down inside
18 even though I don't like to admit it, I'm jealous Jake, Clay,
19 and Jenny had my dad around their whole life while I
20 didn't.
21 ANNIE: That would be hard.
22 TORI: I don't hate his kids, my brothers and sister, it's just ... he
23 was my dad first. You know? But they got more of him
24 than I did.
25 ANNIE: That must be hard.
26 TORI: Yeah ...
27 ANNIE: I wonder if my dad realizes how hard it is for me to see
28 him hang all over some girl who's only a few years older
29 than me. And besides that, my parents have only been
30 divorced a few months. But there my dad is acting all
31 playful and silly with her. Heck, you'd think he was a
32 teenager. It's really disgusting.
33 TORI: At least my dad is past that stage. I'm not even sure if he
34 and Jill are all that happy anymore. But I don't think
35 either one of them would want to go through a divorce.

1 ANNIE: Well, I look forward to the day my dad is past his
2 infatuation with Lacy. My brother and I agreed to have
3 dinner with them last week and it was sickening to watch
4 them. You should have seen them! They couldn't seem to
5 sit close enough. And they sure couldn't keep their hands
6 off each other!
7 TORI: What does your brother think about the situation?
8 ANNIE: Matt will hardly talk about it. I think he's afraid to get
9 on Dad's bad side, but you can tell he's holding a lot of
10 feelings inside. But the truth is, Matt isn't the same fun-
11 loving brother that I always knew.
12 TORI: I guess he'll be forced to do the every-other-weekend
13 visit at your dad and Lacy's house, huh?
14 ANNIE: Yeah. As least I won't have to deal with that.
15 TORI: I remember how hard it was for me to adjust to the
16 weekend visits with my dad at his new apartment after he
17 and Mom divorced. But right away, Jill was always around.
18 At first, Jill tried to impress my father by playing games
19 with me, but all I wanted to do was spend time with my
20 dad. Alone. But she was always around. Then, when
21 things settled down, Dad always stuck me in front of the
22 TV and popped in a movie. That way he and Jill could have
23 their alone time.
24 ANNIE: I guess that's one reason I should be glad I'm older now
25 that my parents have divorced.
26 TORI: Yeah. And then when I came home from a weekend with
27 my dad, my mom always interrogated me. "What did you
28 do? Did he treat you OK? Did he yell at you? Did he feed
29 you anything besides junk food? Did his girlfriend come
30 over? Did she spend the night? She didn't, did she?"
31 ANNIE: No visitation for me. I don't think I'll ever go to Dad and
32 Lacy's house.
33 TORI: If you do, it will be strange at first. Seeing your dad at a
34 new house, with his new wife ...
35 ANNIE: Make that *young* wife.

1 TORI: Laughing, sneaking kisses, acting like, well, not acting
2   like your dad.
3 ANNIE: Oh, and would you believe that Lacy is wearing a white
4   wedding dress to the courthouse to get married? I mean,
5   who does that?
6 TORI: So this is her first wedding?
7 ANNIE: Yes. But it's not my dad's first wedding!
8 TORI: I know.
9 ANNIE: My dad has already been down this path! With my
10   mom! And they were married for over twenty-five years.
11 TORI: Twenty-five years? Wow. That is a long time. Especially
12   nowadays.
13 ANNIE: Yeah, twenty-five years. And Dad has already been
14   through the babies, diaper changes, learning to ride the
15   bike, driving a car ... He even got to see me, his firstborn,
16   graduate from high school a couple months ago. My gosh!
17   What is he thinking? He should be thinking about having
18   grandkids, not becoming a newlywed and starting all over
19   again!
20 TORI: Well, you can't really blame Lacy for that.
21 ANNIE: No, I do blame Lacy! She should have told my dad no
22   when he made advances toward her! She should have told
23   him he was too old for her! She should have found a man
24   her own age!
25 TORI: I agree with you, Annie, but there's nothing you can do
26   about it now. And you know, eventually your mother will
27   move on too. Mine did.
28 ANNIE: Oh, that's a lovely thought. And knowing my mom,
29   she'll hook up with some guy her own age. Which means
30   next year I could breeze through the kitchen in my pj's
31   and find some strange bald headed-man sitting at the
32   kitchen table drinking coffee with my mother. You know
33   what, I'm not doing this!
34 TORI: *(Laughs.)* I'm sorry, I don't mean to laugh, but that was
35   funny. I doubt your mom will move on that fast. Although,

1   with your dad getting married so soon ...

2 ANNIE: I think she will go that fast. As a matter of fact, she's

3   been talking to someone on the phone a lot ... with her

4   bedroom door shut. Which it's not normal for my mother

5   to go into her bedroom, shut the door, and talk on the

6   phone for hours and hours.

7 TORI: Sounds like she may be moving on then.

8 ANNIE: I can't even imagine Mom with some other man.

9 TORI: My stepdad, Mike, has been more of a father to me than

10   my own dad.

11 ANNIE: Probably because you were young when your parents

12   divorced. But it won't be that way with me. I'm not

13   bonding with some old man I don't even know! And I'm

14   not accepting Lacy as my new stepmother!

15 TORI: Maybe you and Lacy can become friends. You know,

16   hang out.

17 ANNIE: What? Hang out and go shopping at the mall with my

18   dad's new wife? And do what? We both head over to the

19   juniors department and find clothes that we both like? No

20   way!

21 TORI: But if they eventually have kids —

22 ANNIE: That's not even a thought I can handle right now.

23 TORI: They probably will. Especially since Lacy is so young and

24   this is her first marriage. Surely she'll want kids.

25 ANNIE: This is too much! Just the thought! You know what,

26   Tori, the only thing I will accept is for my dad to come to

27   his senses and come back home.

28 TORI: But your parents are divorced, Annie.

29 ANNIE: Then they can get back together! I'm sure if he begs my

30   mom for forgiveness she'll take him back. I'm sure deep

31   down inside she still loves him. And maybe Dad was just

32   going through a midlife crisis!

33 TORI: I'm sure all that's possible, but —

34 ANNIE: I know, I know, its just wishful thinking.

35 TORI: I think it's normal for kids to want their parents to

1   reconcile. Even at our ages.

2 ANNIE: I guess.

3 TORI: I used to try to get my parents back together, but it never

4   worked. I once wrote them notes and signed each other's

5   name. Not only did it not bring them back together, but it

6   forced me to sit through two agonizing lectures.

7 ANNIE: OK, I know I have to accept this.

8 TORI: I'm afraid that's true, Annie. Somehow, someway, you've

9   got to wrap your head around the fact that your parents

10   are moving on. And your dad is getting married next

11   week.

12 ANNIE: Yes. Because he's in love!

13 TORI: In love or in love with the idea of being in love,

14   whichever it is, you can't change what's about to happen.

15 ANNIE: No, but it still makes me sick to my stomach.

16 TORI: So you're not going to the wedding next Friday?

17 ANNIE: No.

18 TORI: What about your brother?

19 ANNIE: Matt will probably go just to keep Dad happy. But I

20   refuse. And I refuse to go to their new house and swim in

21   their pool as Dad has already suggested a million times.

22 TORI: So what are you going to do? Never speak to him again?

23   You can't do that.

24 ANNIE: Why not? I'm sure Mom won't. She hates him and I

25   don't blame her.

26 TORI: Do you hate him?

27 ANNIE: Yes. *(Pause)* No. I mean, I don't know.

28 TORI: You hate what he's doing, but you still love him.

29 ANNIE: I love the dad I had before he left us. But I hate the dad

30   he's become and what he's done to Mom.

31 TORI: That's understandable.

32 ANNIE: Therefore, I won't go to his stupid wedding. And he and

33   Lacy can just pretend his previous family doesn't exist as

34   they start a new one.

35 TORI: I heard second marriages only have a fifty percent

1   chance of surviving.

2 ANNIE: I don't care.

3 TORI: Or you could do the opposite.

4 ANNIE: What do you mean?

5 TORI: You could suddenly become daddy's little girl who calls

6   him all hours of the night ... and day.

7 ANNIE: What do you mean?

8 TORI: You need help with this. You need help with that. You

9   need advice. You have a flat tire. You need a ride here. A

10   ride there. You drop by unannounced and throw pool

11   parties at their new house. And how could he say no to

12   you? After all, he wants you to be happy and accept his

13   new wife ... your new stepmother. Not to mention the guilt

14   he feels for leaving his family.

15 ANNIE: *(Chuckles.)* Oh, that's good. I give Lacy the stepdaughter

16   she didn't know she wanted. And just wait until she sees

17   what she's married into! A ready-made family!

18 TORI: Huge fights are on their way!

19 ANNIE: Talk about a honeymoon being over!

20 TORI: Dad, spend time with *me!*

21 ANNIE: Dad, let's hang out! Just the two of us!

22 TORI: Dad, I want to live with you and Lacy!

23 ANNIE: Oh, she'd hate that!

24 TORI: I bet!

25 ANNIE: And I can be a very messy person. Clothes all over the

26   floor. Dishes here, dishes there. The sink? Are you kidding

27   me? I leave them wherever I want! Let the maid pick up

28   my mess!

29 TORI: They have a maid?

30 ANNIE: No. But I guess Lacy can be my maid.

31 TORI: And I'd be more than happy to come over on a regular

32   basis and make myself at home.

33 ANNIE: Yes, and all my friends will be invited over as well.

34   Anytime. Day or night. My house, well, Dad's house, is

35   your house.

1　TORI: The two lovebirds won't have a moment to themselves.
2　ANNIE: Lacy wants my dad, well, guess what? She's getting my
3　　　　dad and a teenage daughter and all her friends and all our
4　　　　drama to go with it. Dad already said he thought I should
5　　　　attend junior college for the first couple of years, and I
6　　　　have to live somewhere, don't I? So, he and Lacy can have
7　　　　me!
8　TORI: This is too good!
9　ANNIE: You know, instead of a fifty percent chance to succeed,
10　　　　I'd say this marriage has a ninety-nine point nine percent
11　　　　chance to fail!
12　TORI: Hard to feel sorry for the guy ... marrying a girl half his
13　　　　age.
14　ANNIE: I'd say he's getting what he deserves.
15　TORI: So are you going to the wedding now? So you can become
16　　　　daddy's clingy little girl?
17　ANNIE: I should, but, I mean, it was a nice thought.
18　TORI: But you can't?
19　ANNIE: No. I can't support what he's doing.
20　TORI: I don't blame you. I wouldn't, either.
21　ANNIE: It's sad. Our parents don't even realize the hurt they've
22　　　　caused us because of their broken promises.
23　TORI: Till death do us part.
24　ANNIE: To heck with that.
25
26
27
28
29
30
31
32
33
34
35

21. The Interrogation

Cast: DETECTIVE HANSON and KATE
Setting: Interrogation room

1 HANSON: I need you to answer my questions.
2 KATE: I have nothing further to say.
3 HANSON: I understand you're upset.
4 KATE: I'm not upset. But I'm tired of you asking me a million
5   questions!
6 HANSON: But you haven't answered my questions.
7 KATE: Yes, I have! You just don't like my answers.
8 HANSON: I want to hear the truth, Kate. We need to get this
9   settled.
10 KATE: Settled? Is that your way of saying that you need me to
11   confess?
12 HANSON: It would help.
13 KATE: I'm sure it would help you. Because then you could wrap
14   this up and go home. But that's not going to happen. I'm
15   not going to confess to anything!
16 HANSON: Let's go over this again. Did you or did you not enter
17   the residence at two twenty-two Maple Avenue at
18   approximately eleven ten p.m.?
19 KATE: I want an attorney!
20 HANSON: Answer the question. Again, did you or did you not
21   enter the residence at two twenty-two Maple Avenue at
22   approximately eleven ten p.m.?
23 KATE: I did not.
24 HANSON: Why are you lying?
25 KATE: You can't prove that I did anything!
26 HANSON: We have witnesses.

1   KATE: Who?

2   HANSON: The owner of the home with a bullet in his chest, for

3   one.

4   KATE: He didn't see me.

5   HANSON: He?

6   KATE: Or she. Because I wasn't there!

7   HANSON: We have your fingerprints.

8   KATE: Not mine.

9   HANSON: Again, did you or did you not enter the residential

10   address of two twenty-two Maple at approximately eleven

11   ten p.m.? *(Silence)* And did you or did you not fire a

12   weapon with the intention to kill the owner of the home?

13   KATE: No!

14   HANSON: And did you or did you not take a large amount of

15   cash from the desk drawer?

16   KATE: No!

17   HANSON: Even though your fingerprints were discovered

18   throughout the house.

19   KATE: Look, my uncle lives there! So of course you're going to

20   find my fingerprints at his house!

21   HANSON: So you broke into your uncle's home tonight?

22   KATE: No!

23   HANSON: Then what were you doing with all that money?

24   KATE: What money?

25   HANSON: The money that was found in the glove compartment

26   of your car.

27   KATE: I don't know how it got there!

28   HANSON: Kate, do you expect me to believe that you always

29   drive around with twenty-five hundred dollars in your

30   car?

31   KATE: Believe what you want! But I didn't take it!

32   HANSON: Then who did take it?

33   KATE: How would I know? But I didn't do it!

34   HANSON: How many times are we going to have to go over this?

35   Did you or did you not enter the residence —

1 KATE: I want an attorney!

2 HANSON: You will be appointed an attorney in the morning.

3 KATE: Well, until then I'm not answering any more questions!

4 HANSON: It would be to your benefit if you would cooperate.

5 KATE: I am cooperating! You just don't like my answers!

6 HANSON: What were your plans for the money you stole from

7   your uncle?

8 KATE: Oh, I don't know. Let's see ... I guess I was going to catch

9   the next flight to Paris. You know, start a new life.

10 HANSON: Why?

11 KATE: Because this stupid town has no culture! Besides a

12   movie theatre, what do we have here? Museums? Live

13   theatre? Art shows? Concerts? No! Nothing!

14 HANSON: So you admit that you took the cash to leave the

15   country?

16 KATE: No! I'm not admitting to anything!

17 HANSON: Were you going to leave the country by yourself?

18 KATE: Probably. You know those plane tickets to Paris can be

19   quite expensive. Then I would need some spending

20   money when I got there.

21 HANSON: So do you admit —

22 KATE: No!

23 HANSON: And what about your uncle?

24 KATE: What about him?

25 HANSON: Are you not worried about his condition? I believe

26   he's in surgery as we speak.

27 KATE: Well, I was planning to go to the hospital and check on

28   him once you let me go. So, can I leave now?

29 HANSON: No.

30 KATE: You can't hold me in here like a prisoner! I want to leave!

31 HANSON: You're not leaving, Kate.

32 KATE: Why not? You don't have any evidence against me!

33 HANSON: We have plenty of proof. We'd just like to have your

34   confession as well.

35 KATE: But I didn't do it!

1 HANSON: That's not what your getaway driver said.

2 KATE: I told you Christy and I were just out driving around! No

3   crime in that, is there?

4 HANSON: With twenty-five-hundred dollars in your glove

5   compartment?

6 KATE: I told you, I don't know how the money got there!

7 HANSON: Christy told us everything, Kate.

8 KATE: You're lying, Detective Hanson! She didn't! She wouldn't

9   tell you anything!

10 HANSON: Yes, she did. She told us how you made her wait

11   across the street as you snuck into your uncle's home at

12   approximately eleven ten p.m. She said she sat in your car

13   and waited for you and then she heard a gunshot. That's

14   when you ran out of the house with a handful of money

15   and ordered her to drive away as fast as she could. So, are

16   you telling me that Christy is lying? Is she? Is she lying?

17   Tell me!

18 KATE: Stop it! Stop asking me these questions!

19 HANSON: And Christy told us how you stuffed the money into

20   the glove compartment. Then you told her to drive to an

21   all-night diner so you could figure out what to do next.

22   That's where the police caught up with you.

23 KATE: They had no business searching my car!

24 HANSON: And isn't it ironic that your uncle was missing

25   twenty-five hundred dollars? All in one hundred dollar

26   bills. And guess how many one hundred dollar bills they

27   found in your car, Kate? Twenty-five. How do you think

28   that's possible? So you see, Kate, it's time for a confession.

29   Did you or did you not —

30 KATE: No!

31 HANSON: Kate —

32 KATE: No!

33 HANSON: We have the proof. We have Christy's confession and

34   we have your uncle, who as I said is in surgery as we

35   speak, who was able to tell the officer that it was you, his

1   niece, who broke into his home. So tell me, Kate, why
2   would you shoot your uncle?
3   KATE: I didn't ... I mean ...
4   HANSON: You didn't? Then who did?
5   KATE: It was an accident, OK?!
6   HANSON: It was an accident? You accidentally shot your uncle
7   as you stole twenty-five-hundred dollars from his desk
8   drawer?
9   KATE: No, it wasn't like that! He snuck up from behind me and
10   it scared me! I don't know, I just turned around and I ...
11   HANSON: Shot your uncle in the chest?
12   KATE: It was an accident!
13   HANSON: I see.
14   KATE: And I wasn't stealing his money! I was borrowing it!
15   HANSON: Borrowing it?
16   KATE: Yes!
17   HANSON: Borrowing it for what, Kate?
18   KATE: To leave this stupid town! I told you that!
19   HANSON: And where were you going?
20   KATE: Were you not listening to me? I was going to catch a
21   flight to Paris! I told you that!
22   HANSON: And what about Christy? Was she going with you?
23   KATE: Christy didn't even know what was going on until I ran
24   out of my uncle's house. When she saw me stuff all those
25   hundred dollar bills into my glove compartment, she
26   freaked out and started screaming at me. Then she
27   started crying. I knew she'd cave. Even though she
28   promised me she wouldn't.
29   HANSON: So you're telling me that when Christy drove you to
30   your uncle's house she had no idea what you were about
31   to do?
32   KATE: That's right. I just told her to wait in the car while I ran
33   in to get something. She didn't know anything.
34   HANSON: That appears to match her statement. But we are
35   continuing with our investigation.

1 KATE: Look, you let Christy go home! None of this was her
2   fault! She didn't know I planned to take ... to *borrow* some
3   money from my uncle. She had nothing to do with it!
4 HANSON: And what about Phil?
5 KATE: What?
6 HANSON: What about Phil?
7 KATE: I don't know what you're talking about.
8 HANSON: Was Phil not waiting for you outside your uncle's
9   house?
10 KATE: I have nothing further to say!
11 HANSON: And was it not Phil who pulled the trigger when your
12   uncle entered the room and caught you two stealing his
13   cash?
14 KATE: No! I was the only one in the house!
15 HANSON: We brought him in for questioning.
16 KATE: Why? My boyfriend doesn't know anything about what
17   happened tonight!
18 HANSON: Why are you trying to cover for him? Especially when
19   he's the one who shot your uncle?
20 KATE: You don't know that! Were you there?
21 HANSON: Christy said you told her it was Phil who entered the
22   home with you. You were carrying the flashlight and he
23   was carrying the gun.
24 KATE: That's not true!
25 HANSON: And when your uncle flipped on the light switch,
26   Phil shot your uncle.
27 KATE: No! It was me! Phil wasn't even there! Why are you trying
28   to bring my boyfriend into this?
29 HANSON: So whose idea was this?
30 KATE: It was my idea! It was all my idea! OK?!
31 HANSON: But he wanted to help you, right? So he borrowed his
32   father's gun —
33 KATE: I didn't say that!
34 HANSON: Like you borrowed your uncle's money?
35 KATE: I told you I was going to pay him back!

1 HANSON: Did you ever think about just asking your uncle for
2   the money?
3 KATE: No. My uncle wouldn't have given me the money.
4 HANSON: So you decided to rob your own uncle?
5 KATE: I wouldn't put it that way, Detective Hanson!
6 HANSON: So tell me, Kate, was Phil going with you to Paris?
7 KATE: We were going to Canada.
8 HANSON: And Phil didn't mean to shoot your uncle, right?
9 KATE: No! It was an accident! I told you that!
10 HANSON: I see. And you just needed to borrow a little cash to
11   get away, right?
12 KATE: That's right! I was just going to borrow the money and
13   after Phil and I got to Canada and found jobs we were
14   going to pay him back.
15 HANSON: I see.
16 KATE: So you understand?
17 HANSON: I do. I understand.
18 KATE: Well, thank goodness! I'm relieved to hear that!
19 HANSON: But I still need your confession to wrap this up.
20 KATE: Then I can go, right? We'll all be released?
21 HANSON: I'll have to check on that.
22 KATE: Because I promise we didn't mean to do any harm. Phil
23   and I just needed some money to get out of here.
24 HANSON: I understand. So, on March eighteenth, at
25   approximately eleven ten p.m., did you break into your
26   uncle's home at two twenty-two Maple Avenue?
27 KATE: Yes.
28 HANSON: Along with Phil?
29 KATE: Yes.
30 HANSON: And did you pry open the locked drawer of your
31   uncle's desk and take twenty-five-hundred dollars?
32 KATE: Yes.
33 HANSON: And when your uncle heard noises and turned on
34   the light, did Phil shoot your uncle in the chest?
35 KATE: On accident.

1   HANSON: Yes or no?

2   KATE: Yes.

3   HANSON: And then the two of you ran out of the house?

4   KATE: Yes.

5   HANSON: Phil took off running down the street while you
6   jumped in your car as Christy drove away?

7   KATE: Yes.

8   HANSON: And you hid the twenty-five hundred dollars in the
9   glove compartment of your car?

10 KATE: Yes.

11 HANSON: And you told Christy to drive to Kip's Diner and
12   that's where you told her what had happened tonight?

13 KATE: Yes.

14 HANSON: Thank you.

15 KATE: Detective Hanson, can I leave now?

16 HANSON: Kate, I'm sorry, but you can't.

17 KATE: Why not? You got the confession you wanted!

18 HANSON: Because you're in a lot of serious trouble, Kate.
19   Armed robbery, murder —

20 KATE: Murder?

21 HANSON: Your uncle died on the operating table.

22 KATE: What?

23 HANSON: We'll be moving you into another room soon.
24   Actually, into a cell. It shouldn't be too long.

25 KATE: He died? My uncle died? But this wasn't supposed to
26   happen! It was an accident! Do you hear me? It was an
27   accident!

28

29

30

31

32

33

34

35

22. The Wish

Cast: JASMINE and BRITTANY
Setting: A chapel

1   *(At rise, JASMINE stands nervously in front of a microphone,*
2   *speaking at a funeral. BRITTANY stands to her side.)*
3   **JASMINE: I just wanted to say ...** *(Pause)* **I hope I don't cry.**
4   *(Pause)* **I'm sorry.** *(Composing herself)* **OK. Well, as most of**
5   **you know, Brittany was my best friend.** *(Pause)* **Wow. This**
6   **is hard. Really hard.** *(Pauses, takes a deep breath.)* **OK.**
7   **Brittany was like the other half of my heart. She knew**
8   **everything about me. And I mean** *everything.* **She knew**
9   **when to knock some sense into me or when to just be**
10   **there and say nothing. Like when I was fourteen and I**
11   **decided to start smoking. Brittany, well, she was in my**
12   **face reading me the riot act. I mean, who can enjoy a**
13   **cigarette with your best friend griping at you the entire**
14   **time? So I quit. Yeah, I'm glad I did. And then there was**
15   **this time in ninth grade when my dog died. Bojo was his**
16   **name. Bojo was one of those ugly dogs that you couldn't**
17   **help but love. He had this crooked little tail that wagged**
18   **all the time. Black and gray straggly hair that didn't know**
19   **which direction to take. And this horrible habit of licking**
20   **you to death. But all that said, Bojo was the best dog ever.**
21   **And when I talked to him, his little head would tilt to the**
22   **side as if he understood exactly what I was saying. And**
23   **when he died ...** *(Pause)* **Brittany was there. Which was**
24   **good because I was inconsolable. I screamed, cried,**
25   **slammed my fists into the pillows ... I could barely**
26   **breathe. But Brittany, she didn't say a lot. She just handed**

1   me tissues and placed her hand on my back to let me
2   know she was there. *(Pause)* I wish she were here right
3   now.
4   BRITTANY: Why don't you tell them about the day we stopped
5   talking?
6   JASMINE: If only I could go back —
7   BRITTANY: It's too late now.
8   JASMINE: To the day I left. I don't remember the exact day.
9   BRITTANY: June twelfth.
10 JASMINE: But it was in the summer. Shortly after graduation.
11 BRITTANY: The end of our friendship.
12 JASMINE: See, I had to get out of this town. I had dreams to
13   follow.
14 BRITTANY: Did you find them?
15 JASMINE: But even though I left, I never forgot the promise
16   Brittany and I made to each other in the seventh grade.
17 BRITTANY: Best friends forever!
18 JASMINE: Best friends forever.
19 BRITTANY: Then you left. Barely said good-bye.
20 JASMINE: So I went off to California to chase after my dreams.
21 BRITTANY: And I stayed here. Junior college. Empty smiles as I
22   forced myself to make new friends. But no matter who I
23   met, no one seemed to understand me the way you did.
24   You understood everything about me. I could tilt my head
25   to the side like Bojo and you knew exactly what I was
26   thinking. We could look across the classroom and
27   practically engage in an entire conversation without even
28   speaking.
29 JASMINE: I was sure I'd be discovered! I'd arrive in Hollywood
30   and the world would suddenly stop in their tracks and
31   notice me. "She's here!" they would say, "A star has
32   arrived!"
33 BRITTANY: Junior college was OK. I liked the freedom. Shorts,
34   tank tops, flip-flops — no problem. Miss a class? No one called
35   my parents. Pass a note? Who cared? I was growing up.

1 JASMINE: And then I discovered the world was a much bigger
2   place than I'd imagined. I was barely scraping by. Working
3   as a waitress was incredibly hard. And the most
4   disappointing part about it was the tips. Very few people
5   tipped well. And the worst tippers, they were so
6   demanding. "Waitress! Over here! Over here!" No one ever
7   looked at my nametag. My name was either Waitress! or
8   Hey You! Almost every day I had a moment. You know, one
9   of those moments when you go into the bathroom and you
10   look at yourself in the mirror. Holding back the tears.
11   Giving yourself a pep talk. I was so determined. But it was
12   so hard.
13 BRITTANY: And every day as I drove to my classes at the
14   college, I'd pass by our old high school. I'd say it was
15   bittersweet. Our laughter seemed to jump out of the
16   windows. Some days, I yearned to step back in. Roaming
17   the halls again, sitting in the classes, being that silly girl
18   all over again ... but I couldn't. I had been forced to move
19   on. High school was over. And my best friend in the whole
20   world was gone.
21 JASMINE: I was too proud to pack it up and come back home.
22   "Don't give up," I told myself. "You will be discovered! You
23   will find acting jobs!"
24 BRITTANY: But the months seemed to drag by. Nothing
25   exciting happened anymore. School, studying, work ... I
26   needed direction.
27 JASMINE: And let me tell you, the competition was
28   unbelievable! At every turn there was a prettier girl. And
29   she always seemed to have more experience and more
30   talent. It was always the same old story. I had the wrong
31   hair color. I was too short. I was too tall. Too fat. Too
32   skinny. Too this! Too that! And slowly, my dreams were
33   beginning to fade.
34 BRITTANY: So I applied for a job at the local bank. And guess
35   what? They hired me! This would be my first real job.

1   Unless you counted the summers I worked as a lifeguard

2   or baby-sat the Donham children. But this, this was a real

3   job!

4   JASMINE: And then finally, I had a break! A callback. Granted,

5   it was for a small part, but it was something.

6   BRITTANY: Yes, this job was going to give me a new outlook on

7   life.

8   JASMINE: So what if I didn't have any speaking parts? I was

9   sure my acting skills would be noticed as I moved behind

10   the nurses' station. This minor part was going to be my

11   foot in the door! Finally!

12   BRITTANY: The bank is where I met Ricky. He had come in to

13   open a checking account. He was a few years older than

14   me. New in town. And when he asked me out – my heart

15   flip-flopped like a dozen times. I told my coworker,

16   Chrissy, he was the one! I just knew it!

17   JASMINE: But it was just small parts here and there. Walk on.

18   Walk off. Stand in the distance. Part of the crowd. A

19   nobody, really.

20   BRITTANY: And for the first time in over a year, I felt as if I had

21   a best friend again. Finally. Someone who could know

22   what my eyes were saying. Someone who could make me

23   laugh harder than ... than I'd laughed in a long time.

24   JASMINE: So I was working as a waitress, running to this call,

25   that call. The rejection. The disappointment. Wondering

26   if I would ever get my big break. And then it happened!

27   BRITTANY: Ricky asked me to marry him! Of course I said yes!

28   JASMINE: Finally, a speaking part! But not just a few lines. No!

29   I had pages and pages to memorize! Finally! My big break!

30   BRITTANY: My flowers? I chose roses and daisies. Romanic,

31   huh?

32   JASMINE: It was a love story and I was the main character's

33   love interest!

34   BRITTANY: And right away I found this gorgeous wedding

35   dress! Strapless with an elegant train with pearl and

1   crystal beads.

2   JASMINE: Set on a tropical island. Who could ask for more than

3   that?

4   BRITTANY: It would be an outdoor wedding at Carlisle's

5   Botanical Garden.

6   JASMINE: Sandy beaches, palm trees ...

7   BRITTANY: Surrounded by an amazing array of flowers. Lilacs,

8   tulips, baby's breath, daffodils, lavender, blue bonnets ...

9   JASMINE: And I imagined my leading man would not only

10   romance me in the movie, but in real life. Yes, we would

11   fall in love in front of the camera as well as behind the

12   scenes.

13   BRITTANY: Ricky and I were in love. And we were planning the

14   most beautiful, amazing wedding ever.

15   JASMINE: Yes, my leading man and I would quickly fall in love

16   and become the next famous legendary couple. Put us up

17   there with Vivien Leigh and Clark Gable, Elizabeth Taylor

18   and Richard Burton, Lucy and Desi ... Jasmine and ... and

19   whatever his name was. Maybe Leonardo DeCaprio. Or

20   Johnny Depp. Yes. Jasmine and Johnny. Yes, that sounds

21   good.

22   BRITTANY: Ricky and I decided to write our own wedding

23   vows. Do you want to hear mine?

24   JASMINE: And true, I was lacking much experience in the love

25   department. My only experience was in high school. Corey

26   Chapman. Brittany said he wasn't my type. But I didn't

27   listen to her. Besides, I never had a type before.

28   BRITTANY: My vows went like this: "Ricky, thank you for being

29   everything to me. Our future is so bright with the

30   promises we are making today. And Ricky, I promise to

31   always be there for you ...

32   JASMINE: Corey was hot and cold. You know, the kind who's

33   there and then who's not. He'd call and want to see me

34   and I would be so ecstatic. Then he wouldn't call for two

35   weeks and I'd be the most miserable person to be around.

1   And every time Corey did this to me, Brittany would tell
2   me not to waste another tear on a jerk like him. She always
3   had good advice. She was the more sensible one while I
4   was all over the place. And yeah, Corey Chapman, he was
5   a jerk.
6 BRITTANY: "And Ricky, I promise to cherish and care for you,
7   comfort you, encourage you, respect you, and most of all,
8   love you for all eternity. As my friend, my lover, and my
9   husband."
10 JASMINE: But it never happens the way you expect, does it? The
11   movie was what they called a B movie. Low budget. Bad
12   script. I heard it's rated B for bad.
13 BRITTANY: I was so afraid I'd forget my words. But thank
14   goodness I didn't. The wedding was beautiful. Almost like
15   a fairy tale. Except ... except for one thing.
16 JASMINE: No one saw the movie. And I'm glad no one saw it. It
17   was an embarrassment.
18 BRITTANY: It was who I chose for my maid of honor. Janelle.
19   Ricky's sister.
20 JASMINE: Then there were the commercials. At least it paid
21   rent.
22 BRITTANY: Janelle was OK, but it wasn't supposed to be that
23   way.
24 JASMINE: And I started wishing I could go back ...
25 BRITTANY: It should have been Jasmine.
26 JASMINE: Because Brittany could always make me feel better.
27   And I missed how we could laugh about the most
28   ridiculous things.
29 BRITTANY: Best friends forever.
30 JASMINE: And growing up hadn't been as exciting as I'd
31   imagined.
32 BRITTANY: But now I was moving on.
33 JASMINE: If only I could go back.
34 BRITTANY: And oh ... my sweet Ricky. Till death do us part. Till
35   death ...

1 JASMINE: But I sure didn't want to come back for this! Not for
2   Brittany's funeral.
3 BRITTANY: At least you came.
4 JASMINE: It makes me want to press the rewind button.
5 BRITTANY: Yeah, it's true. We couldn't wait to grow up.
6 JASMINE: We thought we were unstoppable.
7 BRITTANY: Look at us, world! Here we come!
8 JASMINE: If only I could do it over. Maybe I wouldn't have left.
9   Or at least stayed in touch.
10 BRITTANY: Why didn't you?
11 JASMINE: I wanted out of this place.
12 BRITTANY: And now I'm gone.
13 JASMINE: And now ... Brittany's gone. And you know what's
14   funny? Well, it's not funny, but it's odd. I couldn't wait to
15   run off and chase after my dreams and now, now I just
16   want to go back to where it all started.
17 BRITTANY: Introduction to algebra. You sat behind me.
18 JASMINE: I sat behind her. *(Laughs.)* I was terrible in math!
19 BRITTANY: Jasmine was terrible in math!
20 JASMINE: I couldn't solve a math problem if my life depended
21   on it! But Brittany, bless her heart, she tried so hard to
22   explain it to me.
23 BRITTANY: Pay attention, Jasmine. You see, algebra uses letters
24   called *variables* to represent any value in a given formula.
25 JASMINE: I still don't get it. What is *x*? What is *y*? But you know
26   what I remember the most? Brittany and I whispering
27   secrets to each other when Mr. Miller wasn't looking.
28 BRITTANY: Hey, did you hear about Kaylee and Matt?
29 JASMINE: No! What?
30 BRITTANY: They did it!
31 JASMINE: They did?
32 BRITTANY: Kaylee told Ashley and Ashley told me!
33 JASMINE: Are you serious? I can't believe it!
34 BRITTANY: I know! And I don't even see those two together!
35 JASMINE: I know! Me either! Yeah, that's what life is all about —

1   *(Laughs)* **Mr. Miller's algebra class!**

2 **BRITTANY: You know what I heard? I heard you should live**

3   **your life so that you don't have regrets.**

4 **JASMINE: And my biggest regret ... my biggest regret was not**

5   **holding onto my friendship with Brittany.**

6 **BRITTANY: Jasmine and Brittany, best friends forever!**

7 **JASMINE: Best friends forever. If I could just have one more**

8   **chance to talk to her ...**

9 **BRITTANY: I'm listening.**

10 **JASMINE: I would tell her ...**

11 **BRITTANY: What?**

12 **JASMINE: I'm sorry. I was selfish. I wish I could change things.**

13 **BRITTANY: I wish you could change things, too.**

14 **JASMINE: Like if I could click my heels three times.**

15 **BRITTANY: Like a in a fairy tale?**

16 **JASMINE: Or wished hard enough.**

17 **BRITTANY: Is that possible?**

18 **JASMINE: Then I wouldn't be standing here in front of this**

19   **microphone at my best friend's funeral.**

20 **BRITTANY: Try it.**

21 **JASMINE: And instead of you lying in a coffin behind me ...**

22 **BRITTANY: I'd be standing next to you.**

23 **JASMINE: If only ... if only I could close my eyes and make a**

24   **wish ...**

25 **BRITTANY: I'll wish with you. Come on! We can do this!** *(Pauses.*

26   *She closes her eyes, and then smiles.)* **I can see you.**

27 **JASMINE:** *(Closes eyes.)* **I can hear you. You're whispering in my**

28   **ear. But I don't understand.**

29 **BRITTANY: I don't want to be dead.**

30 **JASMINE: This isn't real. This isn't real. This isn't happening ...**

31   *(Opens eyes.)*

32 **BRITTANY: Did you hear that? Mr. Miller is telling us to work**

33   **on simplifying variable expressions. Do you want me to**

34   **help you?**

35 **JASMINE: I heard there was a terrible car accident.**

1   BRITTANY: It's not that difficult. Remember, you have to
2   identify any like terms. Like terms are terms that have the
3   same variable with either the same power or exponent.
4   JASMINE: A head-on collision.
5   BRITTANY: *(Whispers.)* Do you want to hear a secret?
6   JASMINE: There was a drunk driver going the wrong way. Ran
7   right into you. And you both instantly ...
8   BRITTANY: When you truly believe it, your wish will come true.
9   *(Long pause. JASMINE closes her eyes, takes a deep breath,*
10   *then opens her eyes.)*
11   BRITTANY: Do you want to hear a secret?
12   JASMINE: Sure.
13   BRITTANY: *(Smiles at JASMINE.)* Ricky and I are expecting a
14   baby.
15   JASMINE: What?
16   BRITTANY: We're having a baby.
17   JASMINE: What? I ...
18   BRITTANY: In May.
19   JASMINE: *(Looks around at her surroundings.)* Brittany?
20   BRITTANY: Yes?
21   JASMINE: That's wonderful! Oh, it's so wonderful! And it's so
22   good to see you again!
23   BRITTANY: It's good to see you, too! *(They embrace.)*
24
25
26
27
28
29
30
31
32
33
34
35

23. Forgiveness

Cast: BLAIR and ALLIE
Setting: Outside a restaurant in Los Angeles
Props: hat, sunglasses, paycheck, paper, pen

1   *(At rise, ALLIE is wearing a hat and sunglasses and stares*
2   *straight ahead. BLAIR enters and stands next to ALLIE.)*
3   **BLAIR: I wonder where my ride is? Guess your ride is late, too,**
4   **huh? Taxis are expensive. My friend Jess is picking me up.**
5   **I work at the restaurant here. But not today. Today is**
6   **payday. Needed my check, you know? Jess said she'd turn**
7   **the block a few times and then pick me up. Guess she**
8   **stopped to check something out. Or probably ran into**
9   **O'Malley's for a chili cheese dog. Yeah, Jess loves to eat.**
10   **I'm always bringing her food home from The Villa. She**
11   **loves me for that. I'm a good roommate, wouldn't you say?**
12   **Scrumptious Italian food delivered to her at no cost. A**
13   **perfectly cooked risotto á la marinara. Or spinach ricotta**
14   **cannelloni. Or the mouthwatering roast veal with red**
15   **wine and mushroom sauce. Yum! Or shall I say delizioso?**
16   **Oh, don't think for a minute that I'm the chef who**
17   **prepares those spectacular dishes.** *(Laughs.)* **No, I just bus**
18   **tables. But sometimes there are complaints, wrong**
19   **orders, you know? And we take home the extras. At least I**
20   **do. Yeah, Jess loves me for that.** *(Pauses.)* **Are you waiting**
21   **for a taxi?**
22   **ALLLIE: No. I'm waiting for my driver.**
23   **BLAIR: Your driver? Well, me too. Jess. She's my driver.** *(Looks*
24   *at ALLIE.)* **But I don't think you're waiting on a friend to**
25   **pick you up, are you? You're waiting on your driver, which**

1   means ... well, you're probably someone important. Am I
2   right? *(Pauses.)* OK. You don't have to tell me. Some people
3   don't like to talk much. That's OK. I'm sorry. I talk too
4   much, don't I? So, do you like the food at The Villa?
5   ALLIE: You're a reporter, aren't you?
6   BLAIR: A reporter? No! I told you I work at The Villa.
7   ALLIE: I'm not answering any of your questions.
8   BLAIR: Did I ask you a question?
9   ALLIE: Several.
10 BLAIR: Uh ... I asked if you liked the food at The Villa? What's
11   wrong with that?
12 ALLIE: Just ask me!
13 BLAIR: Do you like the food at The Villa?
14 ALLIE: Not that! That's just a cover. So go ahead. Throw one of
15   your demanding questions my way! Go ahead!
16 BLAIR: Uh ... I'm not sure what to ask.
17 ALLIE: How about this, "How did you feel when Carson left you
18   for a younger woman?"
19 BLAIR: Who's Carson? Is he your husband?
20 ALLIE: Or how about this one, "Do you think this affair will
21   have a negative impact on your career?" You know, I hate
22   it when you reporters play the dumb act!
23 BLAIR: Dumb act?
24 ALLIE: Sneaking over here as if you are an ordinary person so
25   you can get on my good side and bombard me with
26   questions.
27 BLAIR: But I'm not —
28 ALLIE: As I said, I'm not answering any of your questions!
29 BLAIR: OK. *(Pauses.)* Look, I'm sorry that your husband left you
30   for someone else.
31 ALLIE: Your sympathy means nothing to me.
32 BLAIR: My friend Jess was married for about six months when
33   she found out that her husband was ... well, let's just say ...
34   being inappropriate with the new secretary. It broke her
35   heart. *(Pauses.)* Would you like to talk to her when she gets

1   here? She would understand where you're coming from.

2   ALLIE: Why? So I'll spill my guts and then find my quotes

3   plastered across the front cover of a cheap tabloid? No

4   thank you!

5   BLAIR: I'm confused. Why do you think I'm a reporter? You

6   must be someone really famous, huh? *(Looks closely at*

7   *her.)*

8   ALLIE: *(Lowers her sunglasses for a moment.)* Yes.

9   BLAIR: Allie Canton?

10   ALLIE: Who do you work for?

11   BLAIR: I work here at The Villa! You don't believe me, do you?

12   ALLIE: No. No I don't.

13   BLAIR: Wait! Look at this! *(Takes out her paycheck.)* Look! Here's

14   my paycheck! I told you I came to pick it up today. I'm like,

15   so broke.

16   ALLIE: *(Looks at the check.)* Well, maybe you weren't lying then.

17   *(Still looking at the check)* Is that all you get? How do you

18   live on that?

19   BLAIR: I have a roommate. Jess and I split the bills. So it helps.

20   I was living at home until last year, but I figured it was

21   time for me to move out and pay my own way. Become a

22   responsible adult.

23   ALLIE: Well, I am surprised.

24   BLAIR: About what?

25   ALLIE: That you haven't asked me for my autograph. Or begged

26   to let someone take our picture together.

27   BLAIR: Well, that would be fun. I mean, my parents would be

28   impressed.

29   ALLIE: What about your friend Jess?

30   BLAIR: Jess? Well, she's not really into movies. I'm not even

31   sure she'd know who you are.

32   ALLIE: And you?

33   BLAIR: Oh, I'm impressed. Really! But it seems like you have a

34   lot going on right now and I wouldn't want to impose.

35   ALLIE: Thank you.

1   **BLAIR:** I've seen the headlines. *Allie Catches Rock Star*
2   *Husband with Backup Singer. Allies Files for Divorce.*
3   *Allie Fights for Her Man. Allie Admitted to Hospital for*
4   *Depression.* Obviously you can't believe those tabloids.
5   **ALLIE:** A little truth and a lot of lies. I'm not fighting for my
6   man. She can have him!
7   **BLAIR:** Jess didn't want Corey back either.
8   **ALLIE:** Corey?
9   **BLAIR:** Her husband ... well, ex-husband who cheated on her
10   with the new secretary at the Cummins Meat Factory.
11   **ALLIE:** I see.
12   **BLAIR:** She packed her bags and left as fast as she could. I'd do
13   the same thing, too. Except I might pack his bags and
14   make him leave. What did you do?
15   **ALLIE:** Well, I would've kicked him to the curb, but I didn't
16   have the chance. Came home from an interview with
17   Oprah and noticed that he was gone. Packed his clothes
18   and vanished. Not a note or anything.
19   **BLAIR:** What a jerk!
20   **ALLIE:** Yeah.
21   **BLAIR:** Well, it's good you're out having a nice dinner at The
22   Villa. You must be feeling better.
23   **ALLIE:** I had a business meeting with my agent. New movie.
24   Haven't decided if I'll take it or not. Maybe. My agent says
25   it's a great role. But I'm not sure if I'm ready.
26   **BLAIR:** It would probably be good for you to throw yourself
27   into work. Is it an exciting role?
28   **ALLIE:** A drama. I'd play the local District Attorney who
29   prosecutes a group of young men for a brutal crime
30   against a family in Chicago. A few twists and turns. A hero
31   in the end. Emotionally compelling and dramatic. Could
32   be a role of a lifetime. My agent says it has Oscar written
33   all over it.
34   **BLAIR:** That's amazing! So how could you say no?
35   **ALLIE:** *(Shakes head.)* I'm not sure I'm ready.

1   **BLAIR: Because of Carson?**

2   **ALLIE: Yes! Of course because of Carson! He's humiliated me in**

3   **front of the entire world. Discarding me like yesterday's**

4   **trash while flaunting around LA with his new love! Never**

5   **mind me! Never mind the embarrassment and hurt I'm**

6   **feeling.**

7   **BLAIR: That's kind of the way Jess felt. She was humiliated and**

8   **her heart was broken at the same time.**

9   **ALLIE: Yeah, well ... more than that I'm just ... just ...**

10 **BLAIR: Angry?**

11 **ALLIE: Yes. But maybe I should be relieved. Relieved to be rid**

12   **of that tattooed hard rocker. We did clash in so many ways.**

13   **I can't even say I liked his music.**

14 **BLAIR: You know, I can't say I liked it either. And I didn't really**

15   **see you two together. So maybe you should say good**

16   **riddance.**

17 **ALLIE: Yes. I should say that and move on.**

18 **BLAIR: And take that role of a lifetime. Then when you win the**

19   **Oscar for best actress ...**

20 **ALLIE: That's expecting a lot.**

21 **BLAIR: Then you can thank everyone in the world except for**

22   **him. And you will smile into the camera and glow with**

23   **happiness as you hold your award up high, and everyone**

24   **will be focused on you! You could be like, "Thank you,**

25   **thank you so much! I'm so touched and honored by this**

26   **award. First, I'd like to thank my agent who suggested this**

27   **role to me. Thank you ... " What's his name?**

28 **ALLIE: Richard.**

29 **BLAIR: "Thank you, Richard. And to the writers and the**

30   **producers," you know all those people you have to thank.**

31   **"And to Daniel ... "**

32 **ALLIE: Who's Daniel?**

33 **BLAIR: It's the made-up name of the new man in your life.**

34 **ALLLIE: I'm through with men.**

35 **BLAIR: "To Daniel, for your love and support. I love you, baby!"**

1   ALLIE: You're quite an actress yourself, aren't you?

2   BLAIR: Oh no! I don't want to act. But I think that'd be fun. You
3   know, winning the best actress award and thanking the
4   new love of your life.

5   ALLIE: You know, you have made me feel better.

6   BLAIR: I'm glad. *(Offers her hand.)* I'm Blair, by the way.

7   ALLIE: Allie. But you knew that already.

8   BLAIR: I'm glad to meet you, Allie. Seriously, if you ever want
9   to come over and hang out with me and Jess, you're
10   welcome. But I'm sure you have tons of famous friends to
11   hang out with, huh?

12   ALLIE: Actually, no. In this line of business it's hard to have
13   close friends. And then when you're married, you're
14   always with that person. Carson and I were constantly
15   attending this event or that event. When he wasn't on the
16   road, of course. And I guess when he was on the road he
17   was keeping himself occupied with her.

18   BLAIR: And he will have to live with that, won't he? I wouldn't
19   want that guilt on my conscious. And as my mother always
20   said, "your sins will eventually catch up with you." Even if
21   you stuff it and hide it, it will eventually surface.
22   Especially at night when you lie down to sleep. That's
23   when the guilt shows up. Causing you to toss and turn and
24   keeping you awake half the night.

25   ALLIE: Somehow I doubt he's feeling guilty.

26   BLAIR: He will. Trust me. And even if he never tells you he's
27   sorry —

28   ALLIE: *(Half laughs.)* He won't tell me he's sorry! He couldn't
29   even give me an explanation! Not verbally or in a note!

30   BLAIR: Which means you still have to forgive him.

31   ALLIE: Forgive him? Me, forgive him?

32   BLAIR: Yeah! So you can get on with your life and not carry that
33   hate around.

34   ALLIE: But I have every right to hate that man!

35   BLAIR: I know, but it's easier to move on with your life if you

1   find a way to forgive him. So like I had Jess do, pretend I'm
2   your ex and tell me how you feel.
3   **ALLIE:** You're Carson?
4   **BLAIR:** Yes.
5   **ALLIE:** How do I feel? I hate you! That's how I feel!
6   **BLAIR:** Good.
7   **ALLIE:** Good?
8   **BLAIR:** Yeah. You need to get it out.
9   **ALLIE:** Get it out? OK. I hate you! I hate that I ever fell in love
10 with you! I hate that you let me talk about having children
11 while all the time you were carrying on with your backup
12 singer. And for what? For a good time? And do you
13 remember how I completely supported you and your
14 career? Even to the detriment of my own career? How I
15 constantly rearranged my work schedule to accommodate
16 you? And what about all those events I attended with you?
17 Smiling and having my picture taken with a man who was
18 being unfaithful to me? And you did this to me why? For a
19 good time? And was it worth it? Well, I hope so! I really
20 hope so!
21 **BLAIR:** *(After a pause)* Now say that you forgive him.
22 **ALLIE:** What?
23 **BLAIR:** Say that you forgive him.
24 **ALLIE:** I can't do that!
25 **BLAIR:** But it'll make all the difference.
26 **ALLIE:** Why?
27 **BLAIR:** Trust me.
28 **ALLIE:** But I won't mean it.
29 **BLAIR:** Just say it.
30 **ALLIE:** *(Takes a deep breath.)* And you know what? With all of
31 that said ... *(Pauses. She shakes her head.)*
32 **BLAIR:** Come on. Say it.
33 **ALLIE:** With all of that said ... I forgive you, Carson. I forgive
34 you.
35 **BLAIR:** I know that was hard.

1   ALLIE: Yes ... yes, it was.

2   BLAIR: But don't you feel better?

3   ALLIE: Surprisingly I do.

4   BLAIR: It's because you're no longer giving Carson any power

5   over you.

6   ALLIE: Is that what it is?

7   BLAIR: Yes. You can still hate what he did to you, but

8   forgiveness is very powerful.

9   ALLIE: How is it you're so wise in this?

10   BLAIR: *(Smiles.)* Counseling.

11   ALLIE: For what? What happened?

12   BLAIR: A drunk driver plowed into the car my dad and little

13   sister were in. They were on their way to Tessa's ballet

14   class. Dad made it, but my sister ... she didn't.

15   ALLIE: Oh, I'm so sorry!

16   BLAIR: It was a long time ago, but I had a hard time getting

17   over my anger.

18   ALLIE: I can't even imagine.

19   BLAIR: My counselor encouraged me to speak to this drunk

20   driver as if he were in the room. Of course I was only

21   venting to thin air, but it was undoubtedly a powerful

22   experience for me.

23   ALLIE: I've heard of doing that before. Telling a person exactly

24   how you feel, even if they're no longer around. I guess

25   there is something healing about the whole process.

26   BLAIR: There is. And of course it's all about your well-being,

27   not about giving the perpetrator a free pass for hurting

28   you. So that's what I did. I found a way to forgive the

29   drunk who killed my little sister.

30   ALLIE: Does he know you forgave him?

31   BLAIR: Oh, no. I never spoke to him. But it was something I had

32   to do for me. So now I'm able to focus more on the love I had

33   for my sister. And on the good times. Our silliness. Our

34   laughter. She was an amazing little sister. When she was

35   young she called me Sissy. *(Pause)* I still miss her.

1   **ALLIE:** *(Touches her arm.)* **I'm sure you do, Blair.**

2   **BLAIR: But take it from me. You can be happy again.**

3   **ALLIE: You've given me a lot of hope. I actually do feel better**

4   **than I have in weeks.**

5   **BLAIR: Oh, there's Jess! Well, I've got to go. Hey, it was nice**

6   **meeting you, Allie!**

7   **ALLIE: You too, Blair.**

8   **BLAIR:** *(Quickly scribbles on a piece of paper.)* **Oh, and here's my**

9   **number. If you ever need to vent or anything.**

10   **ALLIE: Thank you.**

11   **BLAIR: Sometimes it's a daily thing. You know, forgiving that**

12   **person everyday until the hurt starts to fade. But that's**

13   **OK. Daily. Hourly, if needed. But just do it.**

14   **ALLIE: I will.**

15   **BLAIR: And good luck with that new movie.**

16   **ALLIE: Thanks.**

17   **BLAIR: Bye!**

18   **ALLIE: Bye.**

19

20

21

22

23

24

25

26

27

28

29

30

31

32

33

34

35

24. Reflection

Cast: TITANIA and REFLECTION
Setting: In front of a mirror

1   *(At rise, TITANIA and REFLECTION face each other.*
2   *TITANIA leans forward and REFLECTION does the same.*
3   *TITANIA touches her face and REFLECTION does the same.*
4   *For a moment they stare at each other.)*
5 **TITANIA: Why?**
6 **REFLECTION: Why?**
7 **TITANIA: Why do I hate looking at you in the mirror? I should**
8   **probably remove every mirror in my entire house. Yes.**
9   **That's what I should do.**
10 **REFLECTION: Don't do that.**
11 **TITANIA: You know what you are?**
12 **REFLECTION: Yes. Your reflection.**
13 **TITANIA: You're worthless! That's what you are! No one loves**
14   **you and you know it!**
15 **REFLECTION: I'm worthless and no one loves me?**
16 **TITANIA: Yes! Worthless and unlovable. You hurt and**
17   **disappoint everyone who is important to you.**
18 **REFLECTION: I don't mean to.**
19 **TITANIA: But you do! Look at you!**
20 **REFLECTION: Look at me. I'm your reflection.**
21 **TITANIA: And I hate you.**
22 **REFLECTION: But I'm just an illusion. The light hits the glass**
23   **and the image reflects off of it.**
24 **TITANIA: Exposing every flaw.**
25 **REFLECTION : That's your perception.**
26 **TITANIA:** *(Leans toward REFLECTION.)* **That scar on your chin …**

1   REFLECTION: I fell off the bike when I was five.

2   TITANIA: That red bump on your forehead.

3   REFLECTION: Clumsy me, hit the cabinet door. I thought it was

4   closed, but it wasn't. *(Rubs forehead.)* **That hurt.**

5   TITANIA: And your eyes look dull and lifeless.

6   REFLECTION: They do?

7   TITANIA: And your skin ... why can't it be smooth, soft, and

8   radiant?

9   REFLECTION: I didn't sleep much last night. Tossed and

10   turned.

11 TITANIA: And those stupid freckles.

12 REFLECTION: Some people find them attractive.

13 TITANIA: I don't. I hate them.

14 REFLECTION: I thought they were cute.

15 TITANIA: They're not! And your lips ... I wish they were full and

16   shapely like a model's.

17 REFLECTION: They're not that bad.

18 TITANIA: Yes they are. Everything about you is disgusting.

19 REFLECTION: Why do you always insult me?

20 TITANIA: *(Turns away from REFLECTION.)* **Because I hate what**

21   I see when I look at you!

22 REFLECTION: *(Also turns from TITANIA.)* **Because you only see**

23   what you want to see.

24 TITANIA: I see your flaws.

25 REFLECTION: Everyone has flaws. Flaws make you who you are.

26 TITANIA: Mirror, mirror on the wall —

27 REFLECTION: I'm not playing this game with you.

28 TITANIA: Who's the ugliest girl of all? *(Pause)* **Tell me!**

29 REFLECTION: I told you, I'm not playing this game with you.

30 TITANIA: It's not a game. Mirror, mirror on the wall —

31 REFLECTION: I'm not doing this.

32 TITANIA: Who's the ugliest girl of all?

33 REFLECTION: Why you are, my dear.

34 TITANIA: Thanks! Thanks a lot!

35 REFLECTION: You forced me to say that. Is that what you want?

1   To hear every negative detail about yourself?

2 TITANIA: No.

3 REFLECTION: Then maybe I should tell you all the horrid

4   things since you want to hear them so badly.

5 TITANIA: Never mind.

6 REFLECTION: Mirror, mirror on the wall. Who's the ugliest girl

7   of all?

8 TITANIA: Stop it.

9 REFLECTION: Why you are, my dear. You are the saddest and

10   most pathetic creature I have ever seen. And yes, you

11   should remove every mirror in the entire house. Because

12   who would want to look at you?

13 TITANIA: Stop it!

14 REFLECTION: I'm doing what you asked.

15 TITANIA: Shut up!

16 REFLECTION: Then what do you want from me?

17 TITANIA: I want you to look back at me and ...

18 REFLECTION: And?

19 TITANIA: *(Turns to REFLECTION.)* And reflect someone who is

20   beautiful.

21 REFLECTION: *(Looking at TITANIA)* I'm doing that now, but you

22   won't see it.

23 TITANIA: What do you mean?

24 REFLECTION: You only want to see the bad.

25 TITANIA: How can I not? Look at you! Look at your hair!

26 REFLECTION: *(Touches her hair.)* What's wrong with my hair?

27 TITANIA: What's wrong with your hair? You even have to ask?

28   It's a mess! It's dull and unflattering!

29 REFLECTION: But what if I do this? *(Pulls hair back.)*

30 TITANIA: That doesn't help.

31 REFLECTION: *(Arranges hair another way.)* Or this?

32 TITANIA: That doesn't change anything. You still look the

33   same. Maybe even worse when you do that.

34 REFLECTION: How about if you find something positive about

35   me?

1   TITANIA: That will be hard.

2   REFLECTION: Just one thing?

3   TITANIA: *(Leans forward.)* One thing?

4   REFLECTION: At least.

5   TITANIA: Your nose has a nice shape.

6   REFLECTION: Thanks.

7   TITANIA: It's not crooked or pointy or anything like that.

8   REFLECTION: Something else.

9   TITANIA: *(Takes a deep breath.)* I don't think there is anything
10   else.

11 REFLECTION: Try.

12 TITANIA: *(Leans forward.)* Maybe your lips aren't as bad as I'd
13   thought. They could be worse.

14 REFLECTION: Things are looking better.

15 TITANIA: I wouldn't say that.

16 REFLECTION: I wish you could see what's on the inside.

17 TITANIA: That's not what I'm looking at.

18 REFLECTION: Too bad.

19 TITANIA: I'm looking at you and I don't like what I see.

20 REFLECTION: Because you're too critical.

21 TITANIA: I'm facing the truth.

22 REFLECTION: I disagree.

23 TITANIA: Of course you would. You're just my stupid
24   reflection!

25 REFLECTION: Do you want to hear my thoughts?

26 TITANIA: No.

27 RELFECTION: You did earlier.

28 TITANIA: I wanted you to agree with me.

29 REFLECTION: But when I did, you got mad.

30 TITANIA: I only want my truth. Not yours.

31 REFLECTION: And your truth is ... ?

32 TITANIA: You are worthless and ugly and no one likes you.

33 REFLECTION: No. Deep down inside, I like myself.

34 TITANIA: No you don't.

35 REFLECTION: Yes I do.

1 TITANIA: Mirror, mirror on the wall —

2 REFLECTION: Who's the fairest of them all?

3 TITANIA: What does that mean, anyway? Fairest?

4 REFLECTION: Beautiful.

5 TITANIA: Snow White was the fairest, but you ... you're like the

6   wicked Queen.

7 REFLECTION: No I'm not.

8 TITANIA: Mirror, mirror on the wall —

9 REFLECTION: Who's the fairest of them all? Why you are, my

10   dear!

11 TITANIA: Are you having fun?

12 REFLECTION: Quite. I'm beautiful ... and my flaws ...

13 TITANIA: I hate your flaws.

14 REFLECTION: Are a reflection of my uniqueness.

15 TITANIA: I would argue with you about that.

16 REFLECTION: I know. You argue with me all the time.

17 TITANIA: You can't convince me that you are some unique

18   human being who deserves anything but pity.

19 REFLECTION: I deserve what I believe I deserve.

20 TITANIA: What does that mean?

21 REFLECTION: *(Points to head.)* It all starts here.

22 TITANIA: Are we through?

23 REFLECTION: Sure. I'm feeling much better. Aren't you?

24 TITANIA: *(Stares at reflection.)* No.

25 REFLECTION: Then it's your problem, not mine.

26 TITANIA: No, you are my problem! When I look at you I am

27   disgusted!

28 REFLECTION: Why? Just tell me why!

29 TITANIA: Because I can't do anything right and you remind me

30   of that!

31 REFLECTION: Then concentrate on what you do right.

32 TITANIA: Obviously not much. Not much at all!

33 REFLECTION: Tell me something good that you did this week.

34 TITANIA: There is nothing good. But I'll be happy to tell you the

35   bad stuff. Do you want to hear about it?

1 REFLECTION: No thank you.

2 TITANIA: Let's see, yesterday I lied to my boss. I told him I'd
3 completed a task when I hadn't. That's one reason I
4 couldn't sleep last night. Tossed and turned. Wondering if
5 I'd be found out. Or worse yet, fired.

6 REFLECTION: Then fix it first thing Monday morning.

7 TITANIA: And then I talked bad about my coworker. Ran her
8 right into the ground! Wasn't that nice of me? I guess I
9 thought it'd make me look better, but it didn't. It only
10 made me look worse. "Kendyl has no sense of fashion."
11 Well, look at me! As if I have some fashion statement going
12 on here!

13 REFLECTION: We can work on that.

14 TITANIA: I do good not to mix the wrong colors and walk out
15 the door in a complete clash for the whole world to see!
16 Who do I think I am?

17 REFLECTION: I'm still waiting for something positive here.

18 TITANIA: I ate junk food all day. That was good, wasn't it?

19 REFLECTION: Tomorrow is another day.

20 TITANIA: Oh, and I dropped out of my chemistry class. It was
21 too hard. Way to go, huh?

22 REFLECTION: There's always next semester.

23 TITANIA: And I forgot to turn off the sprinkler last night.
24 Flooded my yard.

25 REFLECTION: Mistakes happen.

26 TITANIA: And no one called me all weekend. Stayed home.
27 Nothing to do. All alone. Wouldn't you say that classifies
28 me as a total reject?

29 REFLECTION: You don't have a phone?

30 TITANIA: I just said no one called me.

31 REFLECTION: Did you call anyone?

32 TITANIA: No, but —

33 REFLECTION: Then I don't want to hear about it. You have no
34 excuses.

35 TITANIA: How can you say that?

1   REFLECTION: That one's on you.

2   TITANIA: Do you want to hear more?

3   REFLECTION: I want to hear about something you did right

4   this week.

5   TITANIA: What I did right? Well, I can't think of anything.

6   REFLECTION: I can.

7   TITANIA: No you can't.

8   REFLECTION: The mall?

9   TITANIA: So I turned in a lost wallet. So what?

10   REFLECTION: The old man at the post office?

11   TITANIA: I opened the door for him. So what?

12   REFLECTION: The sad woman on the elevator.

13   TITANIA: I don't remember a sad woman on the elevator.

14   REFLECTION: You smiled at her.

15   TITANIA: OK. So?

16   REFLECTION: She was really feeling down about herself.

17   TITANIA: I know the feeling.

18   REFLECTION: Do you remember her?

19   TITANIA: Vaguely.

20   REFLECTION: It gave her hope.

21   TITANIA: My smile gave her hope?

22   REFLECTION: It did. Just that one smile made her feel as if she

23   wasn't so unlovable.

24   TITANIA: Then maybe you should smile at me!

25   REFLECTION: OK. You go first.

26   TITANIA: *(Looks at REFLECTION.)* I don't feel like smiling.

27   REFLECTION: *(Looking back at TITANIA)* Force yourself.

28   Pretend I'm that sad lady on the elevator.

29   TITANIA: This is stupid!

30   REFLECTION: Try it.

31   TITANIA: *(After a pause, she gives a slight smile and RELECTION*

32   *does the same.)* There. I did it. Happy?

33   REFLECTION: You can do better than that. Try it again. *(After a*

34   *pause, TITANIA smiles at REFLECTION and REFLECTION*

35   *smiles at her.)*

1 TITANIA: OK, maybe I do feel better.

2 REFLECTION: So do I. Sometimes you need to smile even if you

3   don't feel like it. The emotions will follow.

4 TITANIA: Thanks for the little lesson here.

5 REFLECTION: Glad to have helped.

6 TITANIA: Are we finished?

7 REFLECTION: One more thing ...

8 TITANIA: What?

9 REFLECTION: Mirror, mirror on the wall —

10 TITANIA: Do we have to do this again?

11 REFLECTION: Think about what we just learned.

12 TITANIA: I'm only doing this for you.

13 REFLECTION: Mirror, mirror on the wall, who's the fairest of

14   them all?

15 TITANIA: Why you are, my dear.

16 REFLECTION: Yes. Yes I am!

17 TITANIA: But far, far from being perfect.

18 REFLECTION: I can admit to that. But on the path to becoming

19   better.

20 TITANIA: If you say so.

21 REFLECTION: Because every day is a new day!

22 TITANIA: That was a profound statement.

23 REFLECTION: And true.

24 TITANIA: *(Turns to REFLECTION and stares at her.)* **Every day is**

25   **a new day.** *(Pushes the hair out of her face and REFLECTION*

26   *does the same.)* **Today will be better.**

27 REFLECTION: Positive thoughts.

28 TITANIA: **Positive thoughts.** *(Touches her face and REFLECTION*

29   *does the same.)*

30 REFLECTION: And don't forget ...

31 TITANIA: What?

32 REFLECTION: To smile. *(TITANIA smiles at REFLECTION and*

33   *REFLECTION smiles back.)*

34

35

About the Author

Laurie Allen was drawn to the theatre while performing plays under the legendary drama instructor, Jerry P. Worsham, at Snyder High School. In this small West Texas town, advancing to and winning the State UIL One-Act Competition in Austin was a goal often achieved. The drama department was hugely supported by the community and earned a reputation of respect and awe as it brought home many awards and first place trophies.

Following this experience, Laurie decided to try her hand at writing plays. Her first play, "Gutter Girl," won the Indian River Players Festival of One-Act Plays Competition. With that, she was hooked, knowing she had found her place in the theatre. Now, more than twenty-five of her plays have been published by various publishing companies. Her plays have been performed at many theatres including The Gettysburg College, The Globe of the Great Southwest, The American Theatre of Actors and the Paw Paw Village Players. Her plays for teens have enjoyed wide success with many going all the way to national speech and forensics competitions.

Laurie Allen may be contacted at txplaywright@aol.com.

Order Form

Meriwether Publishing Ltd.
PO Box 7710
Colorado Springs, CO 80933-7710
Phone: 800-937-5297 Fax: 719-594-9916
Website: www.meriwether.com

Please send me the following books:

_____ **Acting Duets for Young Women**   **$17.95**
#BK-B317
by Laurie Allen
8- to 10-minute duo scenes for practice and competition

_____ **Sixty Comedy Duet Scenes for Teens**   **$16.95**
#BK-B302
by Laurie Allen
Real-life situations for laughter

_____ **Thirty Short Comedy Plays for Teens**   **$16.95**
#BK-B292
by Laurie Allen
Plays for a variety of cast sizes

_____ **275 Acting Games: Connected**   **#BK-B314**   **$19.95**
by Gavin Levy
A workbook of theatre games for developing acting skills

_____ **112 Acting Games**   **#BK-B277**   **$17.95**
by Gavin Levy
A comprehensive workbook of theatre games

_____ **Improv Ideas**   **#BK-B283**   **$23.95**
by Justine Jones and Mary Ann Kelley
A book of games and lists

_____ **Comedy Scenes for Student Actors**   **$17.95**
#BK-B308
by Laurie Allen
Short sketches for young performers

These and other fine Meriwether Publishing books are available at your local bookstore or direct from the publisher. Prices subject to change without notice. Check our website or call for current prices.

Name: _____ email: _____

Organization name: _____

Address: _____

City: _____ State: _____

Zip: _____ Phone: _____

❑ **Check enclosed**

❑ **Visa / MasterCard / Discover / Am. Express #** _____

Expiration
Signature: _____ *date:* _____ / _____
    (required for credit card orders)

Colorado residents: Please add 3% sales tax.
Shipping: Include $3.95 for the first book and 75¢ for each additional book ordered.

❑ *Please send me a copy of your complete catalog of books and plays.*

Order Form

Meriwether Publishing Ltd.
PO Box 7710
Colorado Springs, CO 80933-7710
Phone: 800-937-5297 Fax: 719-594-9916
Website: www.meriwether.com

Please send me the following books:

_____ **Acting Duets for Young Women** $17.95
#BK-B317
by Laurie Allen
8- to 10-minute duo scenes for practice and competition

_____ **Sixty Comedy Duet Scenes for Teens** $16.95
#BK-B302
by Laurie Allen
Real-life situations for laughter

_____ **Thirty Short Comedy Plays for Teens** $16.95
#BK-B292
by Laurie Allen
Plays for a variety of cast sizes

_____ **275 Acting Games: Connected**   **#BK-B314** $19.95
by Gavin Levy
A workbook of theatre games for developing acting skills

_____ **112 Acting Games**   **#BK-B277** $17.95
by Gavin Levy
A comprehensive workbook of theatre games

_____ **Improv Ideas**   **#BK-B283** $23.95
by Justine Jones and Mary Ann Kelley
A book of games and lists

_____ **Comedy Scenes for Student Actors** $17.95
#BK-B308
by Laurie Allen
Short sketches for young performers

These and other fine Meriwether Publishing books are available at your local bookstore or direct from the publisher. Prices subject to change without notice. Check our website or call for current prices.

Name: _____ email: _____

Organization name: _____

Address: _____

City: _____ State: _____

Zip: _____ Phone: _____

❑ **Check enclosed**

❑ **Visa / MasterCard / Discover / Am. Express #** _____

Signature: _____   *Expiration date:* _____ / _____
      (required for credit card orders)

Colorado residents: Please add 3% sales tax.
Shipping: Include $3.95 for the first book and 75¢ for each additional book ordered.

❑ *Please send me a copy of your complete catalog of books and plays.*